1000 Selena Gomez Facts

Mera Wolfe

Contents

Introduction

Think you know everything there is to know about about Selena Gomez? Well, think again. 1000 Selena Gomez Facts contains all you could ever wish to know about this popular singer and actress.

Facts about Wizards of Waverly Place, Disney, songs, albums, fashion, food, Barney & Friends, Justin Bieber, boyfriends, movies, famous friends, beauty products, likes & dislikes, career, background, lifestyle, and so much more all awaits in 1000 Selena Gomez Facts.

1000 Selena Gomez Facts

(1) Selena Marie Gomez was born on July 22, 1992 in Grand Prairie, Texas.

(2) Selena Gomez was named after the singer Selena Quintanilla-Pérez. Selena Quintanilla-Pérez was a Texas born Latino singer who became a huge star in the 1990s.

She was hugely popular and famous for her impressive vocal range. She won numerous awards, had great commercial success, and signed with a major label. Selena was known as the queen of Tejano.

Sadly and tragically, Selena Quintanilla-Pérez was murdered in 1995 by Yolanda Saldívar. Yolanda Saldívar was a former nurse who became obsessed with Selena after attending one of her concerts. Saldívar was put in charge of Selena's fan club and chain of boutiques but was found to be stealing money. Selena Quintanilla-Pérez confronted Saldívar about this and was shot dead in a Corpus Christi, Texas motel. Saldívar was found guilty of first-degree murder and sentenced to life in prison with the possibility of parole in thirty years.

The murder of Selena Quintanilla-Pérez was a great shock to her fans and the music industry. It felt as if a great career had been tragically cut short just as it was taking off. Thousands of fans attended the public viewing and mass. Selena Quintanilla-Pérez was buried at the Seaside Memorial Cemetery in Corpus Christi, TX on April 3, 1995. Her family created a foundation and museum in memory and she also received a posthumous Hollywood Star.

After her passing, Selena Quintanilla-Pérez was praised
for being a great role model for the Mexican-American
community.

(3) Selena has two younger half-sisters and a younger
step-brother.

(4) Selena describes herself as third-generation Mexican-
American. She also has some Italian ancestry on her
mother's side.

(5) Selena said her family were very poor when she was
growing up and could barely afford to eat at times.

(6) Selena developed an interest in the entertainment
industry at a young age and began attending auditions as
a child actor around the age of ten.

Her big break came when she was cast in the PBS
children's show show Barney & Friends. Selena played the
character of Gianna from Season 7 to Season 8. The show
revolved around a cuddly purple Tyrannosaurus Rex
named Barney.

(7) While she was appearing in Barney & friends, Selena
appeared in the film Spy Kids 3D and also had a role in
the 2005 television film Walker, Texas Ranger: Trial by
Fire. Walker, Texas Ranger was a long-running vehicle for
the cultish action star Chuck Norris.

(8) In 2007, Selena had a role on Hannah Montana as
Mikayla. Hannah Montana was a Disney show best
known for launching Miley Cyrus on a path to stardom.
Miley played the title character in the show.

(9) Selena's biggest acting break came when she won the

lead role of Alex Russo in the Disney show Wizards of Waverly Place. In the show Selena played a teenage wizard living in Greenwich Village, Manhattan. Selena was fifteen years-old when the show began.

The concept behind Wizards of Waverly Place was to do something different from the usual California based sun and beach Disney type of show - hence the New York location. Wizards of Waverly Place was very popular and made Selena famous.

(10) Selena has known Demi Lovato since they were children.

(11) Selena recorded the theme song for Wizards of Waverly Place.

(12) In 2008, Selena appeared in the music video for the Jonas Brothers' song Burnin' Up.

(13) Selena is a fan of Pilates. Pilates is a form of exercise that focuses on balance, posture, strength and flexibility.

(14) Selena voiced Helga in the animated film Horton Hears a Who!

(15) Selena had a leading role in the direct to DVD sequel Another Cinderella Story. Hilary Duff, another Disney star, was the lead in the first film.

(16) When she was Disney, Selena was eventually part of a band called Selena Gomez & the Scene. Selena apparently wanted the band to simply be called The Scene but the record company wanted her to use her own name.

As a compromise they ended up using both. Selena said

that dubbing the band the 'scene' was meant to be ironic.

(17) Selena signed her first record contract when she was sixteen.

(18) Selena and Demi Lovato appeared together in the 2009 Disney Channel film Princess Protection Program. They also performed a song together for the film. The song was called One and the Same.

(19) A Wizards of Waverly Place television film was released in 2009. The film drew high viewing figures and won an Emmy award.

(20) In 2009, Selena became the (at the time) youngest ever UNICEF ambassador. She was only seventeen at the time.

(21) In 2017, Selena underwent a kidney transplant after being diagnosed with lupus. Lupus is a disease that occurs when your body's immune system attacks your own tissues and organs (autoimmune disease). One of the possible side-effects of lupus is kidney damage. No two cases of lupus are alike so it can be a difficult condition to diagnose and treat. The symptoms can include fatigue, headaches, joint pain, fever, and rashes.

Selena said that her own case came about when she was admitted to hospital with abnormally high blood pressure. Thankfully, the doctors were able to diagnose and treat her condition.

Selena said that her kidneys were pretty much 'done' and that she was suffering from arthritis so it was wasn't very nice at all.

(22) Selena is a fan of green tea and thinks it makes a nice healthy alternative to coffee.

(23) Selena was the first person to have one hundred million followers on Instagram.

(24) Selena is 5'5 tall. That's slightly above average for a woman. Most people tend to assume she is tiny but this isn't the case.

(25) Selena has had three number one albums.

(26) Selena's parents were only sixteen when she was born. They broke up when she was five.

(27) Selena had to have chemotherapy for her lupus. She also had to have emergency surgery when one of her arteries broke due to the kidney transplant. This left her with two scars - one on her thigh and one of her abdomen.

(28) Selena's kidney for the transplant was donated by her friend Francia Raisa. Raisa is an actress known for her roles in Bring It On: All or Nothing, The Secret Life of the American Teenager, and Grown-ish.

(29) Selena's zodiac sign is Cancer.

(30) The name Selena is derived from the Greek "Selēnē" - meaning moon.

(31) Selena is a supporter of the San Antonio Spurs basketball team.

(32) Selena is said to have around fifteen tattoos. Many of them are very small though and difficult to notice.

(33) Selena voiced Mavis Dracula in the 2012 animated comedy film Hotel Transylvania. This film was a big hit (despite lukewarm reviews) and grossed well over $300 million.

(34) Selena eventually earned her school diploma with home tutors. Many child and teen entertainment stars tend to be homeschooled.

(35) Selena attended Danny Jones Middle School in Mansfield as a seventh-grader before moving to Florida to start her Disney career.

In 2019, Selena returned to the school for a visit and chatted to students there.

(36) Selena said that school was quite tough for her. She said that she didn't have many friends in school and ate her lunch alone.

(37) When she left her school in Texas as a kid, one of the teachers asked Selena why she was leaving. Selena replied that she had to go to Florida and make a Disney film. The teacher naturally assumed that Selena was making this up but it was all true!

(38) The three countries where Selena has sold the most albums are the United States, Brazil, and the United Kingdom.

(39) Selena was fluent in Spanish as a kid. She said that she lost her knack to speak the language when she was about seven and regrets this.

(40) Selena said it was only in 2016 that she started working with a personal trainer. She wanted to improve

her stamina and fitness for the busy schedule her music and acting career required.

(41) Selena said that the first big fashion purchase she made when she started earning good money was a Louis Vuitton laptop bag.

(42) Selena said that when playing Alex in Wizards of Waverley Place she was very inspired by Jennifer Aniston's portrayal of Rachel Green on Friends and adopted some of Aniston's mannerisms.

(43) Hundreds of girls tested for the part of Alex in Wizards of Waverly Place before Selena was cast.

(44) Wizards of Waverly Place was sold to sixty-six countries around the world. That obviously made Selena a pretty familiar face in global terms.

(45) Selena's mother used to be her manager but when Selena turned twenty-one she removed her mother from this position and chose a new manager for herself.

This led to a lot of speculation in the media that Selena had ruthlessly fired her mother or fallen out with her but Selena said that nothing could be further from the truth. Selena said she simply wanted to stand on her own two feet and make decisions for herself like an adult. Selena said that her mother totally understood her decision and they remained as close as they were before.

(46) Selena says that her grandparents played a big role in her upbringing and she is very close to them.

(47) Selena made her first music video when she was fifteen.

(48) Selena says she loves listening to retro music from the seventies and eighties.

(49) Selena says her fashion sense is an eccentric mixture of Texas and Hollywood!

(50) Selena says that she loves the scent of eucalyptus and lavender oil.

(51) In 2021, Selena starred in the Hulu show Only Murders in the Building. The show stars Steve Martin, Martin Short, and Selena as three crime buffs who team up to investigate a murder in their New York apartment building.

The show (which is a comic murder mystery) earned very good reviews and was renewed for a second season.

(52) The most critically acclaimed film Selena has been in so far is the 2016 Netflix drama The Fundamentals of Caring. This is a road trip movie and also stars Paul Rudd.

(53) When Selena worked for Disney she was never allowed to go to a premiere or wrap-party unless a parent was there as an adult family chaperone.

(54) Selena was seen visiting Disneyland in Anaheim, California in 2019. She tried to be incognito with a hood but everyone saw it was her. She sampled many attractions - including of course the rollercoaster.

(55) Selena hit the headlines in 2015 when she had an assistant hold her half-eaten cheeseburger while posing for red carpet photographs at the at the KIIS-FM Jingle Ball.

You know you must be a celebrity when you have someone on the payroll to hold your burger!

(56) Selena said she was bullied a bit at school in Texas but it made her a stronger person.

(57) Selena says that she used to have a terrible diet when she was a teenager because the food she liked the most was all the stuff that was bad for you.

(58) One of Selena's nicknames is apparently flacca - Spanish for skinny.

(59) Selena got a helix piercing in 2021.

(60) Selena dressed up as Ghostface from the Scream horror movie franchise for Halloween in 2021.

(61) Selena does hiking and dance cardio to stay fit.

(62) Selena celebrated her eighteenth birthday with a karaoke barbecue.

(63) When Selena first joined Facebook in 2009 she had 350,000 friends. Inside two years that number rose to eight million.

(64) When Selena was a Disney star, her mother still made her do chores around the house and she had to be in bed by 11-30. This was designed to keep Selena grounded. A lot of parents of child and teen stars have said similar things. It is important that the child or teen is not treated like a celebrity at home because otherwise they would end up feeling too entitled and spoiled and have an insufferable ego.

(65) Selena said she was about fifteen years-old when the paparazzi first took an interest in her and began taking sly photographs when she was out and about. Selena said that she (understandably) found this weird and intrusive - especially as she was so young. It was something that was hard to get used to.

(66) The first home that Selena purchased when she became famous was a $2.2 million property in the Tarzana area of California's San Fernando Valley. The house has five bedrooms, eight bathrooms, a swimming pool, and basketball court. In 2014 Selena sold the house to fellow pop star Iggy Azalea.

(67) There were stories in 2014 about Selena dating the actor Orlando Bloom but these were never verified or confirmed. Equally unverifiable are more recent stories that Selena was dating the Captain America actor Chris Evans. Though she said she had a crush on Chris Evans the dating whispers were never confirmed or proven.

The gossip may have simply been a consequence of people noting that Chris Evans had started following Selena on Instagram.

(68) Selena celebrated her twenty-third birthday in London. She had tea, cakes, and champagne at the Savoy Hotel before heading out to some trendy night spots.

(69) Selena received a Mickey Mouse charm necklace as a gift from Disney. That must be sort of like the Disney version of someone getting a watch or clock from their company when they retire!

(70) Selena's first kiss was with Dylan Sprouse on Disney show The Suite Life of Zac and Cody. She was twelve

years-old at the time.

(71) A poll by YouGov America found that 93% of people had heard of Selena Gomez.

(72) One of Selena's nicknames is Selenita.

(73) At the premiere of the premiere of Hotel Transylvania 3: Summer Vacation, Selena wore $21,500 worth of Tiffany & Co. diamonds.

(74) Voters on Ranker have Wizards of Waverly Place as the second best Disney Channel show. The number one spot went to The Suite Life of Zack & Cody.

(75) Alex Russo in Wizards of Waverly Place was originally going to be called Julia O'Malley. They decided at the last minute that Alex Russo sounded better.

(76) Wizards of Waverly Place had a number of alternate titles when it was being planned. These included Disney's Wizards and The Amazing Hannigans.

(77) Selena says she likes long classic dresses.

(78) Selena says she sometimes likes to leave conditioner on her hair overnight.

(79) At the time of writing, Selena is estimated to have a net worth of around $75 million. Some sites put the figure even higher than this though.

(80) In December 2010, Selena began dating Justin Bieber. She was eighteen and still making Wizards when they first started a relationship. Selena and Justin Bieber were sort of like the pop star version of Richard Burton

and Elizabeth Taylor in that they split-up and got back together so many times that people lost count in the end. It is believed that they broke-up for the final time in 2018. Because they were both public figures,

Selena said it was tough to have their relationship and comings and goings put under such scrutiny by the media. She found this media spotlight difficult and stressful.

(81) Selena's first solo album debuted at number 1 on the Billboard 200 chart.

(82) Although she maintains a fairly healthy diet, Selena usually treats herself to Coca-Cola and pizza after a show.

(83) Selena once filmed a pilot for a Lizzie McGuire spin-off show called Stevie Sanchez but Disney decided not to turn this into a series. Lizzie McGuire was a popular Disney show with Hilary Duff.

(84) Selena said in an interview at the time that she was heartbroken when Wizards of Waverly Place ended. She did add though that she was excited about doing new stuff in the future.

(85) Although it was set in New York, Wizards of Waverly Place was shot in Hollywood.

(86) As a couple, Justin Bieber and Selena were known as JELENA in the press.

(87) Joe Jonas unsuccessfully auditioned for the part of Justin in Wizards of Waverly Place.

(88) Wizards Vs Werewolves was the most watched

episode of Wizards of Waverly Place.

(89) After the end of Wizards of Waverly Place, Selena took home her character Alex's prop wand as a momento from her time on the show.

(90) A Wizards of Waverly Place video game was published by Disney Interactive Studios for the Nintendo DS in 2009. A sequel was released in 2010.

(91) Dwayne "The Rock" Johnson made a guest appearance on Wizards of Waverly Place.

(92) The Billie Eilish song Bad Guy was inspired by the Wizards of Waverly Place theme song.

(93) Selena was one of the narrators for 2013 documentary film Girl Rising. The documentary tells the story of nine girls from nine different countries.

(94) Selena is famously generous with her friends. She has picked up the tab for lavish parties and swanky boat trips.

(95) Selena has remained friends with her Wizards of Waverly Place co-stars.

(96) Selena seems to prefer non-fiction books to fiction.

(97) Selena sometimes puts her feet in ice after a concert because they can get sore and swollen from all the dancing.

(98) Because of her heritage, Selena is sometimes dubbed a 'Texican' star.

(99) In 2020, Selena purchased a house in Encino, Los Angeles for $4.9 million. The house has six bedrooms, ten bathrooms, and looks like a hotel resort out the back with trees and a small pool. The house used to be owned by the singer Tom Petty.

Selena is pretty lucky the house is still there because it nearly burned down once when Petty lived there. A fire broke out and the house was fortunate to survive.

(100) Selena, like many singers, avoids menthol candy and cough drops because they can make your throat dry. This obviously isn't great if you have to sing!

(101) Selena turned down a part in the movie High School Musical 3. Her explanation was that she didn't want to be typecast and wanted to be taken more seriously as an actor.

(102) In 2015, Selena purchased a luxury home in Fort Worth, Texas, not far from where she grew up. The house sat on one-and-a-half acres of private land. It is believed that Selena sold the house in the end though.

(103) Selena's family said it can be exhausting following her around on tour but fun too.

(104   8) Princess Protection Program was shot in Puerto Rico. It was the first Disney Channel Original Movie to be filmed there.

(105) Selena turned down the part of Mitchie Torres in the 2008 Disney television film Camp Rock. The part was played by Demi Lovato in the end.

(106) Selena was seen with her friend Cara Delevingne at

a New York Knicks basketball game in December 2021.
They had very good seats right by the court. That's the
advantage of being rich and famous!

(107) Legend has it that the CIA used the Barney &
Friends theme song on a loop to mentally break down
prisoners they were interrogating!

(108) The reason why Stevie Sánchez didn't become a
series is that Disney decided to greenlight Hannah
Montana instead.

(109) Theinterns.net ranked Bad Liar as Selena's best
song.

(110) Selena isn't a fan of her song Come and Get It. She
said it sounded like a Rihanna reject.

(111) In 2010, Selena released a clothing line
collaboration with Kmart called Dream Out Loud.

(112) In 2022, a fan petition proposing that Selena be cast
as Spider-Woman went viral. Spider-Woman (Jessica
Drew) is a character in Marvel comics.

(113) Selena's first Grammy nomination was for her
Spanish language album Revelación.

(114) The first person that Selena ever went to see
perform was Britney Spears.

(115) When they became a couple, Selena and Justin
Bieber made their first public appearance together at the
Vanity Fair Oscar party in 2011.

(116) Selena took on a more grown-up role in the 2013

movie Spring Breakers. This is a crime drama about four college-aged girls on their spring break in Florida. Though it got mixed reviews upon its release, Spring Breakers was later named in the BBC's 100 Greatest Films of the 21st Century in a poll by film critics.

(117) Selena is an advocate of the health benefits of ginger root.

(118) One of Selena's dogs was adopted when she was with Justin Bieber. They were in Canada at the time.

(119) Selena is a fan of breakfast crepes.

(120) Horton Hears a Who! grossed nearly $300 million worldwide.

(121) Selena apparently earned $30,000 an episode on Wizards of Waverley Place.

(122) Selena often uses hair extensions when she is on the stage doing a show.

(123) Selena's three most streamed songs are all collaborations.

(124) Selena says she would describe herself as something of a workaholic. She says she loves having something to do and doesn't even mind juggling more than one project at the same time.

(125) Selena seems to be a fan of hats. She has been seen in Walker hats, beanies, and even a Fedora.

(126) Selena likes Indian food.

(127) Selena has been seen drinking Jarritos. This is a
Mexican soft-drink that comes in fruit varieties. Jarritos
are said to be less fizzy than American soft-drinks. The
word jarrito means "little jug" in Spanish.

(128) Selena has performed on America's Got Talent.

(129) Selena is a fan of Reese's Pieces. Reese's Pieces are a
peanut butter candy introduced in 1977. They became
very popular with the 1982 release of E.T. the Extra-
Terrestrial, in which the candy is featured.

(130) Selena is a fan of Ziti. Ziti is a hollow pasta in the
shape of a smooth tube.

(131) Selena usually has a glass of juice which contains
kale and ginger before she goes on the stage. The drink is
designed to give her an energy boost.

(132) Wizards of Waverly was called Les Sorciers de
Waverly Place in France.

(133) Selena currently ranks thirteenth when it comes to
celebrities in the world with the most Twitter followers.

(134) Selena said that when she was a kid she and her
family experienced some prejudice because of their Latina
heritage. Selena says that this simply made her more
proud of her family background. She said that her
grandparents had a tough time when they came to the
United States from Mexico and took over a dozen years to
get citizenship.

(135) Selena shares her Los Angeles home with a couple
of friends.

(136) Selena has described the relationship between her and her mother as like the characters on the Gilmore Girls.

(137) Selena once said that if she'd never become famous and stayed in Texas she'd probably be married now with a couple of kids.

(138) Selena said that when she didn't get parts as a child actor her mother would console her by saying that the part was destined for someone else and that her time would come.

It can be pretty tough in the world of child actors because there are obviously way more kids auditioning than there are parts. All child actors have experienced rejection at some point or other. They just have to dust themselves down and attend more auditions. This certainly isn't easy though because it can be dispiriting to be rejected at such a young age.

(139) Umusic.co.nz ranked Lose You to Love Me as Selena's best song.

(140) Selena says she has entered rehab more than once to receive treatment for depression and exhaustion.

(141) Selena has her own cooking show on HBO Max titled Selena + Chef. She said she got into cooking during the lockdowns.

(142) Selena said that, contrary to what people might think, Disney put no pressure on the stars of their TV shows to become singers. She said it was purely her own decision to have a singing career.

(143) Selena says that taking the risk of appearing in Spring Breakers made people take her more seriously and opened up a few acting doors in Hollywood.

(144) Despite her fame, Selena said there are blissful days when she goes to the park or to a movie and no one notices her.

(145) Selena said there is no specific path or blueprint to follow when it comes from making the tricky transition from child and teen star to a grown-up actor and performer. She says you just have to try and figure it out for yourself as you get older. That said though, Selena has said that Britney Spears was definitely a big inspiration in the way that went from Disney kid to adult pop star in very successful fashion.

(146) Selena was originally going to be called Priscilla but a cousin took that name six months before she was born. Selena's parents were huge fans of Selena Quintanilla so they settled on the name Selena instead.

(147) Selena is a fan of the romance novel Sundays at Tiffany's by James Patterson.

(149) Selena is a friend of Will Smith's son Jaden.

(150) Selen said it is important not to let fame stop you from being yourself.

(151) Selena said that her main acting instruction from the director on Barney & Friends was simply to keep smiling!

(152) Selena puts vegetables in her blender to make a super healthy drink. She is no fan of juicing though and

does it purely for health reasons.

(153) Selena still occasionally visits the three bedroom house she grew up in during her Texas childhood. Selena says that visiting the house keeps her humble and connected to her roots.

(154) A Buzzfeed article in 2021 ranked Wizards of Waverly Place as the greatest ever Disney Channel show. That's So Raven was in second place.

(155) Selena is the fifth richest former Disney star. Justin Timberlake, Miley Cyrus, Christina Aguilera, and Britney Spears are all wealthier.

(156) Selena featured in a remix of Trevor Daniel's song Past Life.

(157) Selena says that Revival was very influenced by Christina Aguilera's album Stripped.

(158) Selena featured alongside Tainy and J Balvin on Benny Blanco's song I Can't Get Enough.

(159) Probably the worst film Selena has been in (unfortunately in this case) is the 2013 car chase thriller Getaway. Selena starred in this film with Ethan Hawke and Jon Voight. Getaway was ravaged by critics (it only has 3% on Rotten Tomatoes) and was a box-office bomb. The only crumb of comfort for the makers of this film is that it didn't cost a fortune to make so their losses were negated somewhat.

Selena suffered the indignity of being nominated in the Worst Actress category at the Golden Raspberry Awards for this movie.

(160) Selena dated Nick Jonas in 2008. This is said to have lasted about a year.

(161) Selena did a UNICEF Benefit Concert in 2013.

(162) Demi Lovato and Selena both began their acting career on Barney & Friends.

(163) Selena Gomez & the Scene had six platinum-selling singles. Selena went solo in 2013.

(164) Selena was the executive producer on the popular Netflix series 13 Reasons Why. She also sang on the soundtrack.

(165) 9.8 million viewers tuned into the Wizards of Waverly Place finale. This placed in the top three most viewed Disney channel shows at the time.

(166) Selena is a fan of the Dr Pepper soft drink.

(167) Selena is a fan of ice pops in the summer.

(168) Selena is a fan of Filipino food.

(169) Selena performed on Good Morning America in 2010.

(170) Selena performed on the French TV show Le Grand Journal in 2015.

(171) Selena guest starred as herself on the Disney series Sonny with a Chance.

(172) Demi Lovato's sister Dallas Lovato was originally going to have a role in Wizards of Waverly Place but she

was axed from the pilot.

(173) Selena's mother said that Selena was about six years-old when she decided she wanted to be an actress.

(174) Selena is said to love Mexican food and fast food but has adapted some of her favourite treats into more healthy options. She likes a breakfast burrito of scrambled eggs, chorizo, avocado, rice, and beans.

(175) On what became known as Blackout Tuesday, Selena chose to devote two weeks of her feed to educational programming created by influential leaders in the Black Lives Matter movement.

(176) Selena was apparently in contention for the lead role in the 2013 remake of Stephen King's Carrie but in the end the part went to Chloë Grace Moretz.

(177) Wizards of Waverly Place premiered to an audience of 5.9 million.

(178) In her first ever Disney audition as a kid, Selena was asked how tall she was and had no idea. Most little kids probably don't have a clue how tall they are!

(179) Selena said that she had to avoid 'teen princess' type roles in order to be taken seriously as an actor.

(180) Selena says it is tough sometimes trying to convince people she is right for a dramatic acting part because she comes with all the baggage of being a famous singer and former Disney kid.

(181) Selena says it is important in life to learn from your mistakes.

(182) In her first ever Disney audition, Selena was asked what her favourite TV shows were and named That's So Raven. She was very shrewd to name a Disney show!

(183) Selena said her advice to young aspiring actors and performers is to stick at it and don't give up.

(184) Selena made a cameo as herself in the 2011 movie The Muppets. Selena was no stranger to the Muppets. In 2008, Selena appeared with Kermit the Frog in a public service announcement for the Association of Zoos & Aquariums' "Year of the Frog" campaign to help preserve frogs and other amphibians.

Selena also featured in a 2008 Disney Channel special with the Muppets.

(185) In 2010, Selena said she wanted to be in a Harry Potter film. Alas though, this didn't happen. The movie franchise was rapidly nearing its end by that point anyway.

(186) Selena says she was a bit of a nerd when she was a kid.

(187) Selena says she actually likes auditioning for movies because if she gets a part she feels like she's got there on merit and wasn't just hired because she's a famous singer.

(188) There were a number of Wizards of Waverly Place children's books to cash in on the success of the show.

(189) Selena had vocal lessons as a kid.

(190) Selena said she always wanted to be both a singer and an actress.

(191) Selena was once diagnosed with food poisoning. She started to feel ill after appearing on The Jay Leno Show.

(192) Late in 2021, it was revealed that Selena now had a rose tattoo on her back. Selena said the tattoo was inspired by her friend Cara Delevingne - who always calls her Rosebud as a nickname.

(193) Selena did a cover of Cruella de Vil for the 101 Dalmatians platinum DVD and DisneyMania 6.

(194) Selena is a fan of the band Paramore.

(195) Selena appeared on Carpool Karaoke with James Corden in 2016.

(196) Selena was involved in the Runway for Life benefit for St. Jude's Children Research Hospital in 2008.

(197) Fancasting sites say that Selena would make a good Domino in a Marvel film. The character is best known as a member of the mutant superhero team X-Force.

(198) Selena's mother remarried in 2006.

(199) Selena seems to like sea food.

(200) Selena has participated in UNICEF clean water appeals.

(201) Selena was cast in Only Murders in the Building because they wanted a younger character alongside Steve Martin and Martin Short to give the show an extra dynamic.

(202) Selena says a diffuser is a tour essential. She likes

the scent of peppermint or lavender to help her sleep.

(203) Selena says that The Heart Wants What It Wants is a very bittersweet song for her because it dredges up memories of a time when she wasn't happy.

(204) Selena says she has a realistic perspective about her early music.

(205) Steve Martin said they were thrilled when Selena agreed to be in Only Murders in the Building because they weren't sure if they'd be able to get her.

(206) Selena is a fan of Goobers. These are chocolate coated peanuts.

(207) Selena has participated in campaigns which encourage young people to come out and vote in elections.

(208) In 2021, Selena was seen to have a Snickers bar in her designer handbag when she was snapped by a press photographer. She obviously likes to have chocolate to hand in case of a craving!

(209) Despite being childhood friends, Selena and Demi Lovato seemed to drift apart as adults.

(210) It is said that Selena once avoided a swanky event at the Met Gala because she knew that Justin Bieber's wife would be there.

(211) Selena said she never gave much thought to her Latin roots until she attended a Latin awards ceremony and heard stories from other attendees about the prejudice they had experienced.

(212) Selena says that London is one of her favourite cities to visit.

(213) Selena said she sometimes drinks beetroot shots for health benefits.

(214) Selena used to have a waterslide at one of her old homes.

(215) Selena is a fan of scented candles.

(216) Selena seems to have faced more criticism than her famous contemporaries when it comes to her singing abilities. This is patently unfair because she has sung live many times and had a long and successful singing career.

(217) It has been estimated that Selena made about three million dollars from her time as a Disney child and teen actor.

(218) In 2020, Selena teamed up with the South Korean girl group Blackpink for the single Ice Cream. Ice Cream debuted and peaked at number 13 on the US Billboard Hot 100, becoming Blackpink's first single to peak inside the top-twenty of the chart.

(219) Selena has been actively involved in the Disney Worldwide Conservation Fund.

(220) In 2020, the Saved by the Bell reboot show received criticism for jokes in the script about Selena's kidney transplant. The producers of the show eventually offered an apology and removed the offending jokes.

(221) Selena said she sometimes avoids looking at her schedule because it often seems intimidatingly busy. She

says it is best just to dive into it rather than worry about it.

(222) Selena has described the Disney factory as a well oiled machine.

(223) Despite its title, most of Selena's Monte Carlo movie was shot in Hungary.

(224) Selena seemed to swap baggy casual clothes for sparkly dresses when she left Disney and became an independent artist.

(225) Selena said she binged a lot of television during the lockdowns.

(226) Selena's clothing line is apparently very eco-friendly.

(227) If her fridge is anything to go by, Selena seems to be a big fan of yoghurt.

(228) When it comes to live action movies, Selena seems to have avoided franchises and CGI blockbusters. This could be by design or simply because she hasn't been asked to be in them.

It would appear to be quite shrewd though to avoid them given that Selena seeks credibility as as an actress and doesn't just want to be a flash in the pan who does a few teen roles.

(229) Wizards of Waverly Place was clearly very influenced by Harry Potter and Sabrina the Teenage Witch.

(230) Baleighsbetterlife.com ranked Sober as Selena's best single.

(231) The producers of Only Murders in the Building said it was difficult to shoot scenes of Selena (in character obviously) walking in the street in New York because people would recognise her and shout out her name!

(232) Selena's wealth is less than that of her ex-boyfriend Justin Bieber. He's said said to be worth well over $200 million.

(233) Selena had to learn how to play polo and do an English accent for her part in the 2011 romantic comedy film Monte Carlo.

(234) Selena thinks that her medical troubles and humble background make her more relatable as a person. Just because she's a rich celebrity it doesn't mean her life is a constant bed of roses or that she's always lived this life.

(235) Selena says she always drinks a lot of water each day to stay healthy.

(236) Demi Lovato and Selena lived together with their mothers in a Los Angeles loft when the girls were young teenagers trying to make it in Hollywood.

(237) The music videos for Selena's songs Lose You to Love Me and Look at Her Now were filmed on iPhone 11 Pro phones.

(238) Selena is a fan of French Brie cheese.

(239) Selena said she never took much interest in elections when she was younger and didn't use her vote.

She regrets that now.

(240) Selena says that when she's at home she loves curling up in a comfy chair by the window.

(241) Selena is a fan of the 1997 television biopic Selena. This movie is about the singer Selena Quintanilla-Pérez - who Selena Gomez (as we noted earlier) was named after. Jennifer Lopez played Selena Quintanilla-Pérez in the film.

(242) Selena says that her weight has always fluctuated.

(243) Selena seems less prone to reinvention than other pop stars. She has never really radically altered her persona or image.

(244) A Barney & Friends TV movie was once banned in Malaysia. It remains unclear why the country took offence to a purple dinosaur!

(245) Selena and a couple of the lead actors in 13 Reasons Why got matching tattoos when production ended.

(246) Selena is yet to tread the boards and do a stage play.

(247) Selena says she has never considered herself to be in competition with or a rival of other former Disney kids like Ariana Grande or Miley Cyrus. She just admires what they've done.

(248) When it comes to cooking, Selena thinks that she could definitely improve her baking skills.
(249) Selena is very fond of wearing black.

(250) Selena likes the smokey eyes look.

(251) Selena says she considers it a great achievement
whenever she makes Steve Martin and Martin Short
laugh on the set of Only Murders in the Building.

(252) Selena has yet to release an autobiography.

(253) Selena has expressed bafflement at the fact that her
kidney transplant has been used for jokes in comedy
shows.

(254) Selena says she is constantly thinking about new
music and lyrics.

(255) Selena is a big fan of tortilla chips.

(256) Selena is a fan of the singer Big Sean.

(257) Selena says she is somewhat addicted to M&Ms and
eats way too many of them.

(258) Popnable ranked Not My Baby as Selena's worst
song.

(259) Selena likes to relax in her garden.

(260) Selena says her hair can get very wild if left to its
own devices. It has to be tamed!

(261) Selena says there is a unique buzz about performing
on stage at a concert. This is probably why most singers
carry on forever.

(262) Selena is a fan of Hitchcock movies.

(263) Selena has an X-Box and Playstation.

(264) Selena is a fan of the actress Nicole Kidman.

(265) Selena seems to prefer having her cold drinks with a straw.

(266) Selena thinks she inherited her good skin from her mother and grandmother.

(267) Selena said that when she worked for Disney she was too young to know anything about contracts or how much money she was getting.

(268) Selena is a fan of cous cous.

(269) Cindy Crawford made a guest appearance on Wizards of Waverly Place

(270) Miley Cyrus was initially cast as Mavis in Hotel Transylvania but was replaced by Selena because of various controversial incidents. Miley was desperately trying to shed her Disney image at the time so Disney executives decided (not unreasonably you might argue) that she probably wouldn't be a great fit for a Disney family movie.

(271) Selena is a fan of the actress Rachel McAdams.

(272) Selena says that her laptop is a tour essential because she likes to watch movies when she has time to kill.

(273) Baleighsbetterlife.com ranked Birthday as Selena's worst single.

(274) Selena loves escape rooms and says she has visited about twenty around the world. These are basically puzzle games where you work as a team. Usually, as the name implies!, you have to escape from a room.

(275) In 2019, Selena took part in a celebrity softball game for charity.

(276) Selena is the executive producer on her HBO cooking show. The show has (at the time of writing) been renewed for a fourth season.

(277) Selena said she was overjoyed to get her first Grammy nomination and cried when she heard the news.

(278) Wolves is Selena's fourth most streamed song.

(279) Selena said one fashion trend she dislikes is shoulder pads. Shoulder pads were more of an eighties thing really.

(280) Selena enjoys watching fans do covers of her songs.

(281) Selena said the thing she loves the most about her native Texas is the people.

(282) Selena's production company was supposed to produce a teen comedy called What Boys Want as a starring vehicle for her in 2009 but this movie never got made in the end.

(283) Selena is a fan of the HBO Larry David comedy show Curb Your Enthusiasm.

(284) Selena was recently announced as one of the judges in the Doodle contest for Google.

(285) Selena says she has never felt entirely confident and satisfied with her music career and still believes she can improve.

(286) The tags on Selena's clothing line have inspirational quotes.

(287) Barney & friends went on a seemingly permanent hiatus as a TV show in the end but the character has been kept alive through various specials and licencing deals.

(288) Selena has been to Chile for UNICEF.

(289) Selena says that growing-up as an only child made her a bit of a show-off and used to the limelight.

(290) Only Murders in the Building was the most watched premiere in the history of Hulu.

(291) If you watch Spy Kids 3D and want to see Selena, she's the kid in the water park scene.

(292) Selena seems to be fond of Leather Band Quartz Watches.

(293) Selena has six rescue dogs.

(294) In 2020, Selena took legal action against the makers of a smartphone game called (The Clothes Forever Styling Game app) for using her likeness without permission. Selena's legal team claimed that one of the characters in the game was taken from a photoshoot she did with Canadian magazine Flare in 2015.
Celebrities earn a lot of money for selling their likeness or name to companies so they obviously don't like it very much at all when a company uses their image for free.

(295) Selena celebrated her 21st birthday at L.A.'s
Bagatelle restaurant. The menu included the Salade
Saesar de Bagatelle, Tuna Tartar, Parisian Gnocchi and
the signature Whole Truffle-Roasted Chicken along with
French fries. There was of course a big cake too.

(296) Selena said a scary movie she loved was the 2010
thriller Frozen. This is about three teens who get trapped
in a chairlift after a day of skiing and must somehow
avoid freezing to death when night falls and the staff have
all gone home.

(297) Selena had a role in the 2016 drama film In
Dubious Battle. The film (directed by James Franco) is
about workers rights during the depression. It did not get
very good reviews.

(298) The Italian fashion designer Stefano Gabbana
caused controversy in 2018 when he called Selena 'ugly'
(in Italian obviously). The created a backlash from
celebrities, fans, and friends connected to Selena. Anyone
who thinks Selena Gomez is ugly probably needs their
eyes tested!

(299) Selena was the biggest Instagram earner in the
world in 2017. She edged out Kim Kardashian West and
Cristiano Ronaldo for that title.

(300) Selena once handed over her Instagram account to
Ruby Bridges so that her followers could learn more abut
racism.

Ruby Bridges was born on September 8, 1954 in
Tylertown, Mississippi. Schools were segregated in the
south at the time but when Ruby was out of (all black)
kindergarten she took an academic test and passed. The

test qualified her to go to an integrated school with white children. Her family were not convinced at first that she should go (they were obviously worried about her safety and racism and protests) but in the end they agreed.

When Ruby went to the integrated school there were indeed protests by racist segregationists and she had to be escorted in and out by US Marshals. At school, she was put in a classroom on her own. Ruby was understandably rather bewildered by all the fuss and attention. She was just a child and didn't understand racism and segregation. In time though school became more normal for Ruby and she joined regular classes. It seems silly and sad now to think there was a time when white and black children were not allowed to take classes together.

Ruby helped to show that children were just children. They were all the same regardless of skin colour. After graduating from high school, Ruby worked as a travel agent for fifteen years.

A TV movie was made about her and she was awarded the Presidential Citizen's Medal in 2001 by President Bill Clinton. When she met President Obama, he told Ruby he wouldn't be in the White House if it wasn't for people like her.

(301) A Chinese TV show once had to offer an apology for doing a parody of the post-op hospital photo of Selena and Francia Raisa after her kidney transplant.

(302) Selena won a Logie Award in 2011 for most popular overseas star. This was for Wizards of Waverley Place.

(303) Selena won a Gracie Allen Awards for Outstanding Female Lead in a Comedy Series in 2010.

(304) Selena has been nominated for several Billboard Music Awards.

(305) Selena said the Versace gown she wore to the 2013 VMAs is one of her favourite fashion moments. She said she felt like an adult for the first time that night.

(306) Selena has a Roman numeral tattooed on the back of her neck.

(307) Selena is said to love popcorn.

(308) Selena is a fan of Saturday Night Live. She has appeared on this show as a guest.

(309) Selena said that she often avoids looking at the discourse on social media because she finds it so depressing. The unpleasantness and disinformation is too much to take.

She is far from the only celebrity to express their dismay at the nastiness and anger on these platforms. Selena has been critical of social media companies for not having stricter guidelines when it comes to online conduct.

(310) Selena is a fan of the film Clueless. This is a 1995 comedy with Alicia Silverstone.

(311) Selena has been in a partnership deal with the sportwear brand Puma.

(312) There has sometimes been speculation that Selena might retire from music to become a full time actor. As of yet though this obviously hasn't happened.

Selena has said on record that she thinks she has plenty of

unlocked potential as an actor and that the best is yet to come when it comes to her acting career.

(313) Selena sometimes drinks olive oil because it is good for her voice.

(314) Selena said that she has religious faith but doesn't like to go on about it too much. She said her faith was a comfort during her medical troubles.

(315) Selena says that she isn't a fan of trendy or obstreperous night clubs and if she does go out she would much rather just go somewhere quiet for a bite to eat.

(316) Selena says she is a big true crime buff.

(317) When it comes to chocolate, Selena is a big fan of Kit Kats.

(318) Though some celebs might want to hide it at the bottom of their CV, Selena says she is proud of her time on Barney & Friends and thinks that it actually taught her a lot about acting and television production.

(319) Selena's official merch shop sells keychains, hoodies, t-shirts, and even vinyl and cassette tape iterations of her music.

(320) Unofficial Selena Gomez merch includes throw blankets, stickers, and coffee mugs.

(321) Selena is believed to have had a brief relationship with Twilight star Taylor Lautner.

(322) Selena says that being famous makes it more difficult to go on dates and find romance because people

have preconceived notions about her.

(323) Selena is a fan of the television show Succession.

(324) Selena has dark brown eyes.

(325) Selena's show size is seven.

(326) Selena said if she could meet any dead celebrity she would choose Marilyn Monroe.

(327) Selena works with the Lupus Research Alliance to heighten awareness of the condition.

(328) Selena is a fan of Chinese food. She said she sometimes even eats leftover Chinese food for breakfast.

(329) Selena is a big fan of Brad Pitt.

(330) Selena is a fan of the movie American Psycho.

(331) Though she is single (at the time of writing), Selena said she would never use a dating app.

(332) Selena is a fan of Drake.

(333) Selena is a fan of video games. She said she played a lot of Grand Theft Auto as a teenager.

(334) Selena is one of only six female artists to have three singles from the same album top the charts – Good for You, Hands to Myself, and Same Old Love.

(335) Selena attended the Vercase Show Milan Fashion Week in 2013

(336) Selena's cars include a Range Rover Sport.

(337) Selena can play the electric guitar a bit.

(338) Selena is a fan of peaches.

(339) Selena said she struggled during the lockdowns because she is used to travelling a lot.

(340) Selena said she never set out to be a role model but is happy to be one if people think she qualifies.

(341) Selena's fashion range Dream Out Loud includes sunglasses and hats.

(342) Selena likes riding her bike for exercise.

(343) Selena is a fan of the horror thriller Ready or Not.

(344) Selena said she had a crush on Jessie McCartney when she was thirteen.

(345) Selena was a spokesperson and partner for Neo by Adidas.

(346) Although she didn't go to a regular school after she left Texas, Selena said her teen years were fairly ordinary in most respects. She had friends and did normal teenager stuff.

(347) Selena is apparently lined up to star in a horror movie called Spiral which is going to be produced by Drake.

(348) Selena is a fan of the comedian and actress Amy Schumer. Amy Schumer has interviewed Selena for a

magazine.

(349) Selena is a fan of dried banana chips.

(350) Selena has supported the Ryan Seacrest Foundation. The Ryan Seacrest Foundation is a non-profit organisation which seeks to improve quality of life for seriously ill and injured children.

(351) Selena says she likes men who are funny and dislikes men who are arrogant.

(352) Selen said that after her parents got divorced she struggled to accept her step-father at first but they became very close in the end.

(353) Selena said that when she was twelve and had to kiss Dylan Sprouse in The Suite Life of Zack and Cody it was sort of embarrassing because she closed her eyes and actually missed his face!

(354) Selena went on vacation to Mexico in 2015.

(355) Selena is a fan of curly fries.

(356) In a poll, YouGov America ranked Selena as the 41st most popular singer of all time. In case you were wondering, the poll was topped by Tina Turner. The poll was more about likeability than sales.

(357) Wizards of Waverly Place was called Magikerne på Waverly Place in Norway.

(358) Selena has used neon eye shadow.

(359) 13 Reasons Why received some criticism for (in the

view of some critics) making depression look glamorous. Selena denied these accusations and said they had simply stuck closely to the book.

(360) Selena says she likes to put her hair in a bun because it gives it a snatched look.

(361) The Russo family in Wizards of Waverly Place were originally going to own a magic shop but the producers changed this in the end because they thought it was a bit too obvious.

(362) The hardware store in Wizards of Waverly Place is named after the show's creator Todd J. Greenwald.

(363) The music video for Baila Conmigo was filmed between Los Angeles, Miami and a fishing village in Brazil.

(364) Selena is a fan of Tatcha. This is a Japanese beauty and skin care range.

(365) Selena briefly dated her Wizards of Waverly Place co-star David Henrie.

(366) Selena's vocal range is mezzo-soprano covering 3 octaves.

(367) Selena is apparently such a fan of lemons she can happily eat them on their own. She says she likes to put salt on them.

(368) The actress and singer Lucy Hale said she is often mistaken for Selena Gomez at airports. They can look quite similar when they have the same hairstyle.

(369) Selena is a fan of San Pellegrino fruit beverages.

(370) Selena said she cringes when she remembers the punkish outfit she wore to the ABC All Star party in 2007.

(371) Selena likes the Dior Hydra Life Triple Impact Makeup Remover.

(372) Though she enjoys a bath, Selena said she is more of a shower person.

(373) Wizards of Waverly Place has an impressive 92% audience rating on Rotten Tomatoes.

(374) Selena is a fan of salsa dancing.

(375) Selena said she had to take the driving test about two dozen times before she got her license. In 2008 she joked that she'll probably hit thirty before she can actually drive.

(376) Selena launched a swimsuit collection with La'Mariette. Selena said she liked the purple costume best.

(377) Selena thinks that when it comes to makeup less is definitely more.

(378) The video for Selena's song De Una Vez has her on a journey through a mystical house.

(379) DJ Snake, Ozuna, Cardi B and Selena Gomez performed the song Taki Taki at Coachella Valley Music and Arts Festival in 2019.

(380) Selena says she likes red lipstick because it is very

old school when it comes to makeup.

(381) Selena says she watches a lot of CNN at home.

(382) Selena says she gets plenty of exercise walking her dogs.

(383) Selena took part in beauty pageants when she was a kid. She said she loved dressing-up.

(384) Selena is a fan of peanut butter.

(385) Selena said that her most treasured possession is her jewelry.

(386) Selena says that her favourite Disney movie is Alice in Wonderland.

(387) Selena once said that when you become famous at a very young age you rather lose track of what normality is actually like.

(388) Selena is a fan of the HBO miniseries The Undoing.

(389) Selena says she doesn't pluck her brows. She only waxes them.

(390) Selena's friend Cara Delevingne will join the cast of Only Murders in the Building in season two.

(391) Selena said that Sydney is one of her favourite cities.
(392) Selena said that one of her big health priorities is to always make sure she gets enough sleep.

(393) Selena is a fan of The Queen's Gambit. This is a

miniseries about a fictional female chess prodigy. It starred Anya Taylor-Joy.

(394) Selena is sometimes called 'Selly' by her friends and family.

(395) Selena signed a $3 million dollar endorsement deal with Pantene in 2015.

(396) Selena is a big fan of scarves and says they make a great fashion accessory.

(397) Selena is (at the time of writing) the sixth biggest female earner on Spotify.

(398) When it comes to all artists, Selena is the 21st biggest earner on Spotify.

(399) Selena described Only Murders in the Building as a dramedy. Translation - it has comedy and drama!

(400) Selena has a music studio at her house.

(401) Selena has a Atea Oceanie dress.

(402) Selena is obviously a big fan of horror movies.

(403) Only Murders in the Building has its own podcast for fans of the show.

(404) Selena likes Derek Rose pajamas.

(405) Selena says she doesn't really know if she is a good actor or not. She says she just does her best.

(406) Selena said the manufactured nature of Disney

television made her yearn for more creative opportunities when she left that part of her life and career behind.

(407) Selena is a big fan of the film The Hunger Games.

(408) Selena's favourite dessert is chocolate cake.

(409) Glamour.com ranked 2017's Bad Liar as Selena's best song.

(410) Selena has been known to visit the Shape House. This is like a sort of health spa where they use infrared technology to make you sweat and release the toxins from your body. It sounds pretty weird but Selena said it has been great for her skin. She said you sweat for about 45 minutes and it basically works like a sauna.

(411) Selena said that she doesn't especially like exercise and running or going to the gym but it's something that she has to do to stay in good condition. Most people will probably have empathy with her because few of us actually like exercise.

(412) Selena is a fan of the Olax SPF lotion.

(413) Selena says she often adds spices or fruit to water to make it more interesting. One of her favourite 'cocktails' is to add lemon, cucumber, mint, and orange to water and drink it with ice.

(414) Selena says she has always known how to make pasta but it was only when she did her cooking show on HBO that she actually learned the correct way to cook it properly!

(415) Over 300,000 concert goers attended Selena's

Revival Tour.

(416) Selena has some KREWE du optic sunglasses.

(417) Selena seems to quite like flared trousers.

(418) Selena seems partial to a turtleneck sweater.

(419) Selena has dined at the New York restaurant which belongs to Lady Gaga's parents.

(420) Selena once rocked a Ulyana Sergeenko mini dress.

(421) Selena said that being part of the Disney 'machine' was like being in the biggest High School in the world.

(422) Selena wore Jimmy Choo shoes to the Hollywood Film Awards in 2015.

(423) Selena said that she covered up the scar from her kidney transplant at first but now she's proud of it and doesn't mind if people see it.

(424) Selena has the number 4 tattooed on her arm. She did this with three other friends - the tattoo a tribute to their gang of four.

(425) Selena has the line 'God Who Strengthens me' tattooed on her hip. This is from the Bible verse Philippians 4:13.

(426) Selena seems to like beige coats.

(427) Selena has a David Koma macrame dress.

(428) Selena said she was encouraged to improvise

dialogue on Only Murders in the Building.

(429) Selena has a Rodarte hoodie.

(430) Selena says she prefers dramas to blockbuster movies.

(431) Selena has a Sybilla dress.

(432) Selena says she would love to do a song with Eminem.

(433) Selena appeared in three episodes of Hannah Montana in total.

(434) Selena is a fan of the ABC show Shark Tank. The show features a panel of investors called "sharks" who decide whether to invest in the business pitch made by entrepreneurs. This is the American version of the Dragon's Den franchise.

(435) Selena appeared on the Disney Channel sketch comedy series So Random! in 2011.

(436) In 2013 there was an hour long Wizards of Waverly Place special called The Wizards Return: Alex vs. Alex. The special had the Russo family visiting Italy. This was not really a feature length television movie but simply an hour long special.

In typical Hollywood fashion they made the film in Los Angeles and just pretended to be in Italy.

(437) Princess Protection Program only took four weeks to shoot.

(438) Selena says that Twizzlers are her favourite candy.

(439) Selena is a fan of the Netflix costume drama Bridgerton.

(440) Selena is a proponent of dialectical behavior therapy. Dialectical behavior therapy (DBT) is an adapted type of cognitive behavioral therapy (CBT).

Its main aims are to teach people how to live in the moment and teach healthy ways to cope with stress, regulate their emotions, and improve their relationships with others.

(441) Selena says that she doesn't act for the fame or money but simply because she loves acting.

(442) Selena said her favourite place to visit in the world is Europe.

(443) Selena and her mother moved to Los Angeles when she was very young to facilitate her aspirations to be an actor. Selena said it wasn't easy at first and they initially lived in a rough part of the city.

(444) Selena says that Price Tag by Jessie J is one of her favourite songs.

(445) Selena is a fan of Stevie Nicks.

(446) Selena said she decided not to appear in the Netflix adaptation of 13 Reasons Why because she was somewhat intimidated by the cult following the book has. In the end she decided she would happier just serving as the producer. Selena felt she might be under too much pressure if she was an actor in the show too.

It could be too that by the time the project went into production Selena had simply aged out of the part earmarked for her. It was originally going to be a movie before it became a Netflix project so it obviously took a while to get to the screen.

(447) Selena was originally supposed to play Hannah Baker in 13 Reasons Why before eventually deciding to simply be the producer.

(448) Selena said that she and her mother couldn't afford to go to Los Angeles for auditions at first when she was a kid so they used to tape her auditions and post them.

(449) Selena's music video for A Year Without Rain was shot on location in Lucerne Valley, California.

(450) Selena had a very small part in the 2012 horror-disaster thriller film Aftershock.

(451) Selena seems to like cat eyed sunglasses.

(452) In 2019, Selena appeared in the Jim Jarmusch zombie horror comedy The Dead Don't Die. The film had a terrific cast (Bill Murray, Adam Driver, Chloë Sevigny, Steve Buscemi, Tilda Swinton, Tom Waits, Danny Glover, Caleb Landry Jones, Rosie Perez, Iggy Pop, Carol Kane) but received mixed reviews. It is probably worth a look if you like horror comedies.

(453) Selena is a fan of the David Fincher film Zodiac. Zodiac was the name given to a killer who operated in California in the 60s and 70s. The Zodiac Killer, who was never found, claimed to have killed thirty people. The police still periodically re-open the case if fresh information comes to light.

(454) Only Murders in the Building is Selena's third television show.

(455) Only Murders in the Building was actually Steve Martin's FIRST television show.

(456) Selena said it was her mother who persuaded her to accept a part in Spring Breakers.

(457) In 2011, Selena had to put a restraining order on Thomas Brodnick. Brodnik was a mentally troubled man alleged to have been stalking her and sending threats. The restraining order meant that Brodnik had to stay well away from Selena. This incident obviously highlighted one of the downsides of being a celebrity.

(458) Selena is sometimes seen shopping for bargains in Target.

(459) Selena said that she loved Steve Martin and Martin Short in the 1986 comedy film Three Amigos! and this made her want to do Only Murders in the Building.

(460) Selena is a fan of chocolate milkshakes.

(461) Selena's Getaway co-star Ethan Hawke did his own stunt driving in the movie - which was a bit nerve-wracking for Selena to say the least!

(462) Selena seems to have studiously avoided musical films - which is obviously shrewd when it comes to avoiding typecasting. She doesn't want to be typecast as a singer or teen star - especially teen star as there is obviously a limited self life to that.

(463) Selena said that her time in the entertainment

industry has made her aware of a dark underbelly to Hollywood.

(464) Selena seems to have remained friends with most (if not all) of her old boyfriends.

(465) Selena is a fan of shopping malls.

(466) Selena enjoys buying music memorabilia.

(467) Selena likes expensive pajamas.

(468) A British tabloid wrote in 2021 that Selena was very worried about money and looking for new revenue streams. It sounded suspiciously like a 'slow news day in the office' clickbait bogus story. It is hard to believe that someone worth tens of millions was seriously worried about money!

(469) Selena has a rock pool at her current home.

(470) Selena likes to take a bubble bath when she has the time.

(471) Selena said it was quite difficult to be a 'Disney kid' at the start of her career because you have to be very careful what you say and how you behave. Hollywood is (sadly) littered with child stars who went off the rails when they grew-up but Selena seems to have coped as well as anyone conceivably could in transitioning from child actor to grown-up star.
(472) The British film publication Little White Lies called Spring Breakers one of the best films of the 2010s.

(473) Wizards of Waverly Place was called I maghi di Waverly in Italy.

(474) Selena likes to have candles in every room of her house.

(475) Selena has addressed graduation ceremonies online. She is especially concerned with the education access of immigrants.

(476) Selena absolutely loves Flamin' Hot Cheetos and says they are a backstage staple when she's on tour.

(477) When it comes to fruit, Selena is a big fan of mangoes.

(478) Selena said she would be more than happy to date someone who wasn't in the entertainment industry.

(479) Selena is a fan of ice cream sundaes. The one she likes best is the Forbidden Broadway Sundae. This contains chocolate blackout cake with vanilla ice cream, hot fudge and whipped cream.

In 2021, Selena created The Selena Sundae for charity (proceeds went to The Rare Impact Fund) through Serendipity 3. Serendipity 3 is a restaurant located at 225 East 60th Street, between Second and Third avenues in New York City. Selena is an investor in this restaurant.

(480) Selena owns a Cadillac Escalade.

(481) Selena has been quite selective with movie roles. She doesn't just do anything that is offered to her. As we have noted, this has been a shrewd and savvy approach. While not all of the films she has appeared in have got good reviews she has taken some risks. This is obviously more conducive to a long acting career than just doing High School Musical type movies.

(482) Selena's Texas home was a bungalow - although a very lavish and spacious bungalow as far as bungalows go!

(483) Selena has the least amount of screen time out of the main female characters in Spring Breakers. She disappears from the movie around the 50 minute mark.

(484) Selena's movie Monte Carlo filmed some scenes in Paris. They did go on location to Monte Carlo at one point but not for very long. It was obviously cheaper and easier to film most of the movie in Eastern Europe.

(485) Some of the names of spells in Wizards of Waverley Place are inspired by members of the crew and the producers.

(486) Selena says her fashion style at home is very casual and not at all glam.

(487) Selena thinks that breakfast is a very important meal. Many of us skip breakfast but Selena thinks it is important to eat in the morning.

(488) Selena stocked up on board games during the lockdowns.

(489) It seems surprising that a person of Selena's compassion and sensitivity has yet to become a vegetarian or vegan. She has supported animal charities but still eats them!

(490) Selena has some Robert Clergerie black leather mules.

(491) Selena has some Gianvito Rossi heeled sandals.

(492) Selena says that one of her idols is the actress Meryl Streep. Selena says she would love to have a long and eclectic acting career like the one that Streep has enjoyed.

(493) Shakira made a guest appearance on Wizards of Waverly Place.

(494) Selena and Justin Bieber once went on a trip together to the West Indies.

(495) Selena likes J Brand jeans.

(496) Selena is a fan of apples.

(497) The Disney movie Another Cinderella Story received some criticism because of the real life age difference between Selena and the male lead Drew Seeley. They play the romantic leads in the movie but Selena was only 15 at the time while Seeley was 26.

Seeley was obviously playing a character younger than his real age but all the same it was deemed to be a bit weird and jarring by some critics.

(498) A video game based on Hotel Transylvania 3 was released but Selena had nothing to do with this project and did not do any voice acting for it.

(499) Selena made a cameo as herself in the 2015 biographical comedy-drama film The Big Short.

(500) Selena is one of the many famous narrators in the 2015 documentary film Unity. The documentary is about the transformation and progress of humans.

(501) Selena's music video for Slow Down was shot in

Paris.

(502) Wizards of Waverly Place won a Nickelodeon Australian Kids' Choice Awards.

(503) Selena's favourite movie when she was a kid was The Wizard of Oz.

(504) Selena said that when she first met Demi Lovato they were both standing in line for the Barney & Friends auditions. There were well over a thousand kids waiting in line for the auditions! That gives you a little insight into how tough and competitive the world of child acting can be.

Selena said that she and Demi passed the time in the queue by doing a colouring book together.

(505) Selena and Justin Bieber were once seen together eating at an IHOP. This is a pancake chain which does breakfasts.

(506) Selena is right-handed.

(507) In 2011, Selena handed out cupcakes to fans who were waiting in a queue for one of her concerts in Canada.

(508) Selena says she doesn't like fragrances that are too strong and over-bearing.

(509) According to Billboard, by May 2017, Selena had sold 24.3 million songs and 3.4 million albums in the US alone.

(510) Some of the characters in Wizards of Waverly Place are named after characters in the vintage sitcom

Bewitched.

Bewitched is an American fantasy sitcom television series that originally aired for eight seasons on ABC from 1964 to 1972. The show starred Elizabeth Montgomery as a witch who marries an ordinary man.

(511) Selena said that one of her great ambitions is to learn more languages. As she travels so much she thinks it would be great if she could talk to more people in their native language.

(512) There were 106 episodes of Wizards of Waverly Place. This makes it the longest running Disney show.

(513) Selena says that she doesn't think she will ever completely banish her anxiety and depression and that coping with it and trying to mitigate the symptoms is an ongoing process.

(514) Selena can play the drums.

(515) Selena is a fan of skating.

(516) There is a twenty-one year age gap between Selena and her young half-sister Gracie. Selena has joked that this is good because she'll be more like a cool older aunt than siblings who are fighting over clothes and boys!

(517) Ranker voted Alex's Brother Maximan as the best episode of Wizards of Waverly Place.

(518) Selena's Back to You music video is a homage to the French film director Jean-Luc Godard. Godard was part of the French New wave movement and directed films like Breathless.

(519) Selena sometimes indulges in a glass of wine after a show.

(520) Selena likes the Spindrift range of soda and seltzer.

(521) Selena is friends with Vanessa Hudgens.

(522) Selena has a Vespa buddy scooter.

(523) Selena was estimated to have a net worth of five million dollars in 2012. This has obviously increased substantially since then.

(524) Selena likes iced tea.

(525) As part of twenty-seventh birthday celebrations, Selena took a group of her friends on vacation to Italy.

(526) Selena is a big fan of the late Audrey Hepburn.

(527) Selena said that her first Disney paychecks were used paying the bills and rent for her and her mother.

(528) Selena is a fan of Bruno Mars.

(529) Selena's favourite colour is green.

(530) Selena does boxing to stay fit - especially when she is in New York. She says she likes to do this in the morning if she can.

(531) Selena considers herself to be an old soul who was probably born in the wrong era. She says she is perfectly happy staying in and curling up by the fire.

(532) Selena said that during the recent lockdowns she

got into watercolour painting.

(533) Selena is alleged to have dated the businessman Samuel Krost circa 2015/2016. Krost owns a luxury clothing company called Krost New York and he has partnered with March For Our Lives to raise awareness about gun violence. He has also appeared in a Netflix documentary.

Selena and Krost were seen having dinner and holding hands at various points. For the record though, Selena denied they were in a relationship and insisted she was happily single at the time.

(534) Selena said her desire to be an entertainer started at a very young age. She said that when she was a kid she put sparkles on her swimsuits so she would stand out more.

(535) Selena said that when she was homeschooled she occasionally missed not being at school with other kids but it wasn't so bad because she was often tutored with other kids on the set of Wizards of Waverley Place so was far from alone.

(536) Selena is a fan of Chili's Grill & Bar. Chili's Grill & Bar is an American casual dining restaurant chain. Her staple order is chips, guacamole, and melty cheese.

(537) When she was about sixteen there was a lot of press about Miley Cyrus and Selena having a celebrity feud because they both liked the same boy. Selena says that this was pure speculation and that they never had a feud. Selena says she is very different to Miley but admires her music.

(538) Selena has said that she is perfectly willing to shed her 'Disney Selena' image for an acting part and would happily shave her hair off if a film required it. I'm not sure her shampoo endorsements would be too thrilled about this!

(539) Selena said she had some anxiety when her Disney days came to an end and she realised she was too old to play the sort of parts that had made her famous. She wasn't quite sure at first what she wanted to do next but - thankfully - music turned out to be a very obvious thing to fall into next and she already had a fanbase from her TV shows. It's not as if she launched a music career as a complete unknown.

(540) Selena was part of the first generation of stars to use the explosion of social media to enhance their career.

(541) Selena has occasionally cut short interviews because she was asked a question about Justin Bieber. This is obviously something she doesn't especially want to discuss these days. The duo have written songs that appear to be about one another since they split up.

Selena was understandably rather sensitive at times to the notion that she was best known for going out with Bieber. She would obviously like to think that there was much more to her life than this.

(542) Selena has worn clothes designed by Victoria Beckham.

(543) Selena said she used to drink a lot of Red Bull and Gatorade but her personal trainer put a stop to this.

(544) Selena says she loves a good old fashioned chicken

pot pie.

(545) It was once reported that Selena earns about $100,000 for a concert.

(546) A website once printed the backstage hospitality rider requested by Selena's team for a concert.

Among the things she requested were Pepper Jack Cheese, turkey breast, tomatoes, lettuce, avocado, mustard, Diet Coke, wheat bread, white bread, fresh fruit, tea bags, and honey. The rider also requested pasta, rice, green vegetables, salad, and potatoes for lunch.

Among the specific instructions were that there should be no Wonder Bread (an American brand of white bread) and that lunch MUST be served with silverware and china. No paper cups and plates for Selena!

One other request was for Clif Bars. Clif Bars are energy bars that come in a range of flavours like peanut butter and chocolate chip.

(547) Selena is a fan of ramen noodles.

(548) Selena said that when she worked with Demi Lovato for Disney the studio usually tried to seperate them and put them in different rooms because they knew they'd stay up all night together talking if they didn't.

(549) Selena purchased her first car in 2013. It cost $34,000.

(550) Selena first met Taylor Swift as a Jonas Brothers concert in 2008.

(551) Selena said she admires Amal Clooney. Amal is George Clooney's wife.

(552) Selena apparently doesn't own a private jet. She does pay for private flights though.

(553) High-interval jump squats are part of Selena's exercise routine.

(554) According to ENews, Selena's gym membership costs $300 an hour!

(555) Selena's Texas home had a putting green. Presumably, the previous owner was a golfer!

(556) Selena once turned up to a swanky event in a $20 dress!

(557) Selena says that when she's seen wearing a fancy expensive dress at a premiere the dress is usually just borrowed from the designer.

(558) Selena is a huge fan of the designer Sami Miró.

(559) Selena has been seen out clubbing in Las Vegas with her friends.

(560) Selena says she likes collecting antiques.

(561) Selena said that Hilary Duff was her idol when she was a little kid.

(562) In 2013, Selena created her own collection of nail polish for Nicole by OPI.

(563) Selena's first tattoo was a tiny musical note on the

wrist of her right hand.

(564) In 2017, Selena played one of the leads in the Woody Allen film A Rainy Day in New York.

A Rainy Day in New York is a romantic picture starring Timothée Chalamet, Elle Fanning, and Jude Law. The film was completed in 2017 but Amazon Studios refused to release the picture in light of the negative publicity Allen had been receiving from Dylan Farrow's ongoing allegations of abuse.

Allen filed a $68 million suit against Amazon Studios alleging the studio had dropped the film for only "vague reasons" and terminated the four-picture contract over "a 25-year old, baseless allegation". The American rights to the film were eventually given back to Woody Allen and plans to release the film in Europe were prepared. It eventually had its premiere in Poland two years after it was made.

Needless to say, the controversy greatly overshadowed the film and so it didn't really do very well or get much of a reception. Selena donated her salary from the film to charity in light of the controversy which (whether fair or unfair) seems to follow Woody Allen these days.

(565) Selena is a fan of avocado toast.

(566) Wizards of Waverly Place was originally going to be set in Ireland but they obviously abandoned this plan in the end.

(567) Selena is a big fan of the 1980s teen movies made by John Hughes. In particular she likes Pretty in Pink and 16 Candles. She said she would love to have been like

Molly Ringwald and starred in those movies.

(568) One of Selena's tattoos is on her ribs. She has the words Love Yourself First written in Arabic.

(569) Selena's own make-up range is called Rare Beauty. Selena said that when she was younger she was quite insecure about her looks ad plastered on too much make-up. She says that as she gets older she is more comfortable in her own skin ad doesn't use as many beauty products.

(570) Selena is a fan of the film director Brian De Palma. Brian De Palma's movies include Carrie, Dressed to Kill, Scarface, Body Double, and The Untouchables.

(571) Selena is a fan of Rihanna.

(572) Selena says she used to enjoy cheerleading when she was younger. This is a big tradition in Texas.

(573) Selena said the meaning behind calling one of her albums Rare is that people today often feel under pressure to all look the same. The subtext of the title is that one shouldn't be afraid to be different - i.e rare.

(574) Selena says she greatly admires the late Princess Diana.

(575) Selena says it has been very difficult to escape from her 'good girl' Disney kid image. She felt that this image was constrictive because it possibly restricted the type of acting work she might potentially be offered.

She is quick to point out that she is very proud of the work she did with Disney but (understandably) just doesn't want her Disney background to overshadow anything else she might go on to do.

(576) Selena said that a beauty trick she learned in her Disney days was to put toothpaste on pimples to banish spots. Dermatologists tend to frown upon this alleged pimple banisher though and say you definitely shouldn't put toothpaste on your skin.

(577) Selena is a fan of Cauliflower Pizza.

(578) Selena's Encino home has a wine cellar and massage room.

(579) The comedian Chris Rock angered Selena's fans in 2016 when he described her as a low-grade Beyonce.

(580) Selena is a fan of Philadelphia Cream Cheese.

(581) Those who have designed clothes with Selena say she is not afraid to venture forth with her thoughts and has strong opinions about fashion.

(582) Selena can do impressions of Shakira and Taylor Swift.

(583) In a YouGov America poll, only 14% of people said they disliked Selena Gomez. 50% of people said they liked her and the rest were neutral and had no firm opinion of her one way or the other.
(584) The production of Spring Breakers was pestered by paparazzi trying to get a photograph of Selena in a bikini. Selena said it was a pretty rough shoot at times.

(585) Selena's lavish house has a spiral staircase.

(586) Selena's house is said to have ten baths. Most of us simply have one!

(587) When she was twenty-three, Selena was named in Forbes 30 under 30. Forbes 30 Under 30 is a set of lists of influential people under 30 years old issued annually by Forbes magazine.

(588) Selena has won an Imagen Award.

(589) Selena has supported the charity Hope for Haiti Now.

(590) Selena has won several German Bravo Otto awards.

(591) Selena teamed with rapper Gucci Mane for Fetish.

(592) Selena owns a Mini Cooper car.

(593) The sales of the album A Year Without Rain are said to have earned Selena nearly a million dollars.

(594) Selena was paid $2.5 million to appear in the film Monte Carlo.

(595) The plush Arcnonia building where Selena's character lives in Only Murders in the Building is fictitious. The exterior shooting location was the Belnord at 225 W 86th St in Manhattan.

(596) Selena's character in the film Getaway was originally called Alex but they changed this because she'd already played a famous character called Alex on TV.

(597) Selena is a fan of the television show Good Girls.

(598) Selena says her favourite karaoke song is anything by Cardi B.

(599) Selena had to train with a stunt car driver to make the movie Getaway and said it was a rather terrifying experience.

(600) Spring Breakers was the first R-rated movie to feature Selena.

(601) It is said that Selena has a strict rule about not doing nude scenes in movies.

(602) Quentin Tarantino said that Spring Breakers was his favourite film of 2013.

(603) Selena is estimated to earn about seven million dollars a year from her music, movies, and business interests.

(604) Selena loves queso. Queso is an appetizer or side dish of melted cheese and chili peppers. It is used as a dip for tortilla chips.

(605) Selena says that the web and social media is full of stories about her that aren't even true.

(606) Selena seemed to imply in one of her interviews that at some point she stopped reading reviews of her music and articles about her because it just makes one feel insecure in the end. She feels that in this specific case ignorance truly can be bliss.

(607) Selena's favourite Latin song is Obtener un Si' by Shakira.

(608) Selena's health and fitness trainer says she will sometimes have Greek yogurt and granola for her breakfast.

(609) Selena says that her favourite fashion trend is skinny jeans.

(610) Selena said she got the showbiz bug from watching her mother prepare for stage productions. Selena's mother dabbled in acting and trod the boards when she was younger.

(611) Selena suffers from farsightedness and has used both spectacles and contact lenses in her life.

(612) Selena says the first CD she bought was Baby One More Time by Britney Spears.

(613) Selena says that strawberries with whipped cream is one of her favourite treats.

(614) In 2018, Selena was diagnosed with bipolar disorder. Bipolar disorder is a mental health condition that causes extreme mood swings. Selena said she was grateful for the diagnosis because it explained the reason for why her moods sometimes seemed to wildly fluctuate.

(615) Lose You To Love Me was Selena's first No. 1 on the Billboard Hot 100 chart.

(616) Selena seems to have suggested that she would be open to a Wizards of Waverly Place revival or reboot.

(617) Selena likes the Nars Lip Pencil.

(618) Selena is a fan of U Luxury Shampoo and

Conditioner.

(619) Selena thinks that shoes are the most important part of any outfit.

(620) Selena says that missing out on being a normal kid was a small price to pay for the life she now leads.

(621) Selena says she likes getting massages.

(622) It apparently took several bowls of bleach and eight hours to make Selena blonde.

(623) Selena said that it was during the fourth season of Wizards of Waverly Place that she started to feel like she had outgrown the show and wanted to do something new.

(624) Selena grew-up in a fairly rural place. She isn't a city girl at heart.

(625) Selena said she would like to do more indie movies. She said she enjoys the creativity and freedom of films that aren't Hollywood blockbusters.

(626) Selena said she is much more comfortable in acting auditions now than she used to be. She said that when she was younger she always worried that she looked too young for parts or lacked specific qualities. She said that over time you learn to stop obsessing about this sort of stuff.

(627) Selena said that she usually tries to separate her Latin heritage from her career because she doesn't want to be judged purely on what she looks like.

(628) Selena said that when it came to acting she tried to

make a gradual transition from Disney to other roles and deliberately didn't do anything too risque or controversial too soon because she wanted to try and bring her Wizards audience along with her as they grew-up too.

(629) Selena uses EOS Moisturizing Shave Cream.

(630) Selena swears by the Sephora cucumber undereye mask. This product only costs $3.50.

(631) Selena said when she was a kid she would only eat broccoli if she was allowed to put cheese on it.

(632) Selena is a fan of the Bath and Body Works Aromatherapy Sugar Eucalyptus Tea Scrub.

(633) Selena likes the Oribe Après Beach Wave and Shine Hairspray.

(634) Selena that her hair can get very wavy and frizzy if left to its own devices.

(635) Selena took part in a virtual show before the 2021 UEFA Champions League Final.

(636) Selena uses the Tarte Maracuja Bronzing Serum when she wants a more bronzed look.

(637) Selena likes the Laura Mercier Oil Free Supreme Foundation in Golden Beige.

(638) Glamour.com ranked Birthday as Selena's worst song.

(639) Selena has the word Sunshine tattooed on one of her feet. This is believed to be a tribute to her

grandmother.

(640) In the music video for Selena's song Love you like a Love Song, horses were spray painted pink. PETA complained about this and so the video was rather controversial. Selena said she didn't know anything about this until she turned up on the set and didn't like it at all.

(641) On Becoming Fearless in Love, Work, and Life by Arianna Huffington is one of Selena's favourite books. This is basically a self-help book aimed at women.

(642) Selena is said to earn hundreds of thousands of dollars for each Instagram post.

(643) Selena has a cream piano in her house.

(644) Selena has a faux fur zebra print coat by Mango.

(645) The top three countries when it comes to accessing Selena's music on YouTube are the United States, Mexico, and India.

(646) Selena has dated The Weeknd - aka Abel Tesfaye. This only lasted for several months though.

(647) Selena is a big fan of Gwyneth Paltrow - both as an actress and fashion icon.

(648) Selena is a fan of carrots and celery.

(649) Selena said she feels at her most creative when she is sad.

(650) In 2022, Selena was voted the seventeenth most beautiful woman in the world by international voters on

the Kingchoice website. The poll was dominated by k-pop stars. Emma Watson was the highest placed western celebrity and came tenth.

(651) Selena says she likes to have at least at hour to herself in the morning before she has to put makeup on and go anywhere.

(652) Selena is a fan of Biore Deep Cleansing Strips.

(653) Selena is a fan of Dr. Dennis Gross Clinical Concentrate Radiance Booster.

(654) Selena is a fan of Three Musketeers candy. This is a chocolate bar with a nougat filling.

(655) Selena can be quite self-deprecating and honest. She once said, for example, that she doubts Miley Cyrus would like her (Selena's) music.

(656) Selena is a big fan of rice.

(657) Selena once visited Nepal for UNICEF.

(658) Selena has the Om symbol tattooed on her hip. This is a symbol of oneness in Hinduism and other world religions. In the west it tends to simply signify peace and spirituality.

(659) Selena says that her ultimate comfort food is fried chicken because it takes her back to her roots in Texas. (660) There is always (unavoidably) a lot of speculation about what celebs have had plastic surgery and which specific treatments they might have undergone. Selena has naturally been a subject in this tittle tattle over the years. Some believe she may have had fillers and surgery

on her nose but this is impossible to verify and could
simply be a natural consequence of her face changing as
she moved from teenager to grown woman.

Selena doesn't look THAT different now from her teenage
self so that is no great evidence of plastic surgery to her
face. There has also been a lot of speculation that she had
breast implants and this seems more plausible because
her figure does seem fuller. It could be though that her
body has changed due to better fitness and diet (plus the
passage of time). Besides, even if Selena has had breast
implants so what? If it makes her feel better then good for
her.

(661) Selena says she likes high heels because they make
her legs look longer.

(662) Selena is a fan of Red Vines candy. Red Vines is a
brand of red licorice candy manufactured in Union City,
California by the American Licorice Company. Red Vines
Original Red Twists are also sometimes referred to as red
licorice despite containing no licorice. The original Red
Vines were cherry-flavored.

(663) Selena's song The Heart Wants What It Wants
spent 20 weeks on the Billboard chart.

(664) Disney shows like Wizards of Waverley Place are
aimed at pre-teens - though of course people of all ages
can enjoy them.

(665) Selena has been known to give flowers to her fans
as gifts.

(666) Selena is one of those celebrities who isn't afraid to
go to ground and duck out of the limelight.

(667) Selena said she likes voice acting because recording studios are pretty plush and comfortable places to hang around. You don't even have to go on location!

(668) Selena is believed to have sold one of her houses and moved as a result of the man who was alleged to be stalking her. In that situation you'd obviously want to move house and go somewhere you felt safer.

(669) Selena was a big fan of Johnny Depp when she was younger. Depp has obviously had his troubles and controversies of late though.

(670) When Selena was sixteen there were stories that she might go to college. She said she'd like to study journalism. Nothing came of this though as she was too busy with her entertainment career.

(671) In 2021, Selena was the most streamed female artist on Indian platforms.

(672) Selena is often cited as the first celebrity to 'blow up' on Instagram and make the platform a popular tool for celebrities.

(673) Selena celebrated her twenty-fifth birthday at her home with family and friends in Los Angeles. She had a pajama party with balloons and cakes.

(674) Selena became an investor in the delivery service app, GoPuff. Selena said she invested in the company after being impressed at how quickly they delivered an order she made.

(675) Selena said that one of her earliest celebrity crushes was the actor Shia LaBeouf.

(676) Carmex is one of Selena's favourite lip balms.

(677) Selena says that one of her most beloved fragrances is Marc Jacobs' Daisy. This fragrance features fruity, strawberry notes.

(678) Selena is a big fan of the Sunset Tower Hotel in West Hollywood. The Sunset Tower Hotel, previously known as The St. James's Club and The Argyle, is a historic building and hotel located on the Sunset Strip. The hotel is a famous landmark thanks to its Art Deco design.

(679) Selena is a huge fan of large hoop earrings.

(680) Selena's nicknames include Selenita and Conchita.

(681) In 2013, Selena received the Chris Greicius Celebrity Award from the Make-A-Wish Foundation.

(682) Selena says that Paris is one of her favourite cities.

(683) Selena is a fan of the late singer Ella Fitzgerald.

(684) Selena Gomez & the Scene sold 85% of their digital units in the United States alone.

(685) Voters on Ranker.Com have Rare as Selena's best album.

(686) In comparison to contemporaries like Ariana Grande and Miley Cyrus, it has been written that there is a palpable lack of mystique about Selena Gomez. Selena seems more of an open book in that what you see is what you get. She seems more approachable and less remote

than other pop stars. You could say that she seems more normal and down to earth.

Ariana and Miley, though both equally nice and pleasant in rel life by all accounts, have more of an elaborate stage image which serves almost like an alter ego. One might argue that Selena has occasionally tried to go against type (so to speak) with things like her Fetish music video but - generally - she's always had more of a girl next door image than many other female pop stars of her era.

(687) Selena uses Drunk Elephant's Umbra Sheer Sunscreen SPF 30 as her daily sunscreen.

(688) It is alleged that Nick Jonas dumped Selena. Though she tends not to refer to him by name she has intimated that this break-up hit her hard and that she took a long time to get over it.

(689) Selena said that when she started her clothing range her main aim was to design clothes that were both comfortable and affordable.

(690) Selena said that occasionally she had some feelings of regret over the fact that she never experienced what it was like to be an ordinary teenager and kid but this is more than mitigated by the fact that she now lives the sort of life that most people can only dream of. She has financial security and a beautiful home.

(691) Selena is a fan of the famous board game Monopoly.

(692) Selena is famously friendly and approachable when it comes to fans and autographs. She will often pose for photographs and sign autographs in fast food places that her team have stopped off at for a bite to eat.

(693) Selena launched her first fragrance in 2012. It was simply titled Selena. In case you are wondering what Selena's fragrance (Selena Gomez Eau de Parfum) smells like - the top notes are Pineapple, Raspberry, Peach and Orange; the middle notes are Blackberry, Freesia and Musk; and the base notes are Dark Chocolate, Vanilla, Coconut and Amber.

The fragrance has been described as floral and fruity.

(694) Selena said she has visited the grave and met the family of the late Selena Quintanilla - the star who inspired her name.

(695) Selena said she never googles herself because she doesn't want to read the nasty critical stuff that might be out there. Sadly, the web seems to bring out the worst in many people.

(696) Selena is pretty rare in that she is a child and teen Disney star but never been involved in any scandal or bad behaviour. Even Ariana Grande (who is super nice) had her infamous donut incident.

(697) Selena's highest rated album on Metacritic is Revelación. This record scored 83%.

(698) Selena is a fan of Ted Gibson's Beautiful Hold hair spray.

(699) Selena used to wear a purity ring which said 'true love waits'. She stopped wearing it around her sixteenth birthday.

(700) Selena will usually play the piano during her

concerts now at some point. She said this was quite nerve-wracking at first. The key to this is to obviously make sure you get plenty of piano practice before you go on tour! Selena says that most days she will try to have a piano lesson.

(701) Selena says that one of her ultimate comfort foods is macaroni cheese. She says another comfort food she loves is her grandmother's dumplings

(702) Selena is said to own over twenty pairs of Converse shoes.

(703) One of Selena's favourite colours is cyan.

(704) Selena is a fan of Urban Outfitter.

(705) Selena is a fan of Sherri Hill clothing.

(706) Selena is a fan of Applebee's. Applebee's Restaurants LLC. is an American company that develops, franchises, and runs the Applebee's Neighborhood Grill + Bar restaurant chain.

The Applebee's concept focuses on casual dining, with mainstream American dishes such as salads, chicken, pasta, burgers, and "riblets" (which is considered Applebee's signature dish).

(707) For her twenty-sixth birthday, Selena had a birthday dinner with her friends on a yacht in Newport Beach. The photographs from the event indicated that a large amount of pasta was on the menu.

(708) Selena said that when she was a child actor her mother used to let her choose her own clothes to wear for

auditions.

(709) Selena said that her years at Disney were positive in terms of acting because she had to learn things like how to deliver a joke and improvisation.

(710) Selena said that when she left Disney and started acting in movies she felt like she starting all over again from the bottom.

(711) Selena said she would love to work with the film director David O. Russell. Her favourite David O. Russell film is Flirting with Disaster. This is a 1996 film that starred Ben Stiller.

(712) Selena said she regrets some of the music videos in which she showed some 'skin' and seemed to be trying to project more of an adult bad girl image.

Selena said that this isn't really her and that she isn't very good at that sort of stuff. It's the sort of thing you'd associate more with Miley Cyrus.

(713) Selena eventually lost her status as the youngest ever UNICEF ambassador when the Stranger Things actress Millie Bobby Brown became a UNICEF ambassador at the tender age of fourteen.

(714) Selena said it is important to her to be in charge of every aspect of her life - both the personal and business sides.

(715) Selena thinks that social media, airbrushed magazine photographs, and celebrity culture can create unrealistic expectations when it comes to beauty and what people think they are supposed to look like.

(716) Selena is a fan of cheesecake.

(717) In 2014, Selena signed with Interscope Records. She recently renewed this deal but her songs are apparently 'under license' to the company. This presumably means that she owns her own catalogue - which is a pretty savvy and rare thing to do.

(718) When she was promoting Only Murders in the Building, Selena made some flippant comments about how she had signed her life away to Disney when she was a kid. Some perceived this to be a rather ungrateful thing to say and Selena was quick to clarify her comment and said she had a great time at Disney and was always well looked after. She said her comment was a tongue-in-cheek sort of quote.

(719) The 55 shows of Selena's Revival Tour grossed around 35 million dollars.

(720) Steve Martin and Martin Short said they became good friends with Selena making Only Murders in the Building.

(721) The Stars Dance Tour was Selena's first solo tour. This tour had to be cut short when she was diagnosed with Lupus.

(722) Selena has performed on the long running and famous British children's television show Blue Peter. This was in 2010.
(723) Selena has done a concert in Japan.

(724) In 2016, Selena broke an Instagram record for the most likes in relation to a photograph. A photo of her sipping Coca-Cola through a straw got four million likes.

Beyonce later beat this record.

(725) Selena was the most followed person on Instagram for more than two years until the soccer player Cristiano Ronaldo overtook her.

(726) Selena holds the record for the most Nickelodeon's Kids' Choice Awards wins.

(727) Courteney Cox, Halle Berry, Tobey Maguire, Jason Derulo, Maddie Ziegler were among the celebrities who attended a July 2016 Selena concert in Los Angeles.

(728) Selena's first live music performance was on Dancing with the Stars in 2009.

(729) Selena sang on The Late Show with David Letterman in 2011.

(730) Bad Liar was probably Selena's best reviewed song.

(731) Selena tends not to view the Selena Gomez & the scene days as a true part of her discography because they operated under a Disney record deal. One can presume that Selena - in retrospect - saw herself as a corporate marketing product rather than an independent artist in those days.

(732) Selena said if she had one wish in life it would be for everyone to be nice.

(733) Selena often seems to express a yearning to be taken seriously as an actress in her interviews.

(734) Selena's two songs at Victoria's Secret Fashion Show in 2015 are considered among her best and most

memorable live performances.

(735) Selena will often have a salad for lunch. This is doubtless a stipulation from her personal trainer!

(736) Selena had something of a leg-up at the start of her music career because Disney have their own radio station. As she was on a Disney label she was guaranteed plenty of airplay.

(737) Music industry sales are increasingly complex to decipher because the industry has gone from CDs to downloads to streams. The general perception is that Selena has done very well but is not quite an A-List top table recording artist when it comes to sheer volume of sales.

(738) Selena said she is not very good with birthdays and doesn't mind if people ignore them.

(739) Selena has a surprisingly deep speaking voice.

(740) Selena thinks that her very round face makes her look younger than she is and has constricted the type of acting roles she might be offered. Though nearly thirty (at the time of writing) she could still pass for a teenager. Selena is hopeful though that she will be able to take on a more eclectic range of roles when she is older.

(741) Selena has gone blonde a few times but usually reverts back to black hair.

(742) Selena's natural hair is quite curly.

(743) Selena is regarded to be one of the more intelligent and articulate former Disney stars.

(744) Selena was in the 2014 music drama Rudderless with the late Anton Yelchin. The film marked the directorial debut of the actor William H. Macy. It got mixed reviews when it was released.

(745) Selena said that the press attention during her time with Justin Bieber was dreadfully claustrophobic in the end.

(746) Selena has been quite shrewd in her movie choices in that she has mostly tended to avoid musical films and family stuff. This is clearly an effort to break free from her Disney image.

(747) Selena seems to be more interested in acting than music these days. Other former Disney stars like Miley Cyrus and Ariana Grande tend to be much more interested in music - though they do occasionally act now and again.

(748) Selena has won several ASCAP Pop Music Awards.

(749) Selena won an Independent Spirit Award at the 2012 Glamour Women of the Year Awards.

(750) Selena won a PETA's Libby Award for her vegan makeup range Rare Beauty.

(751) Selena used to be the most followed woman on Instagram but in 2019 she was surpassed by Ariana Grande.

(752) During her Revival Tour, Selena drew 100,000 people for a concert in Quebec City, Canada.

(753) Selena said she would love to work with the film

director Martin Scorsese. Martin Scorsese has directed classic films like Goodfellas, Taxi Driver, and Mean Streets.

(754) Selena said if she could have one superpower it would be the ability to fly so she could avoid traffic.

(755) Selena said it doesn't really bother her if she doesn't have a boyfriend. She says that relationships are hard work so it's nice to have a spell alone now and again anyway.

(756) Selena is a fan of sushi.

(757) Rao's in New York City is one of Selena's favourite places to eat.

(758) A clip of Selena on Instagram once revealed that she had twelve different types of ice cream in her refrigerator!

(759) Selena and the singer Julia Michaels both got matching hand tattoos as a symbol of their friendship. They both had a small arrow tattoed on their hand.

(760) Selena said she has sometimes felt a frustration in her music career in that she has a sense that people don't take her seriously. This, she speculates, might be an unavoidable consequence of starting life as a Disney kid.

(761) Selena is a fan of Patsy Cline.

(762) Selena is a big fan of cheeseburgers. She definitely hasn't become a vegan celebrity yet.

(763) Selena loves pickles. She said she would love to be

able to buy pickle chewing gum. I don't think that would catch on somehow!

(764) Selena said she got her love of horror movies as a kid when her dad took her to see the movie Seed of Chucky.

(765) Selena says she has learned through experience that it is for the best to keep one's private life private.

(766) Selena is a fan of vodka penne. Penne alla vodka is a pasta dish made with vodka and penne pasta, usually made with heavy cream, crushed tomatoes, onions.

(767) Selena is a fan of Kelly Clarkson.

(768) Selena said she moved house two or three times in recent years because she wanted to find a house that she truly felt comfortable in.

She says that she has never felt comfortable in Los Angeles but her new Los Angeles property has finally made her feel more relaxed and at home in the city.

(769) BestEverAlbums.com ranked Revival as Selena's best album.

(770) Selena used to hold the record for being the female actor with the most Twitter followers. Lady Gaga (though obviously more of a singer) now technically holds this title.

(771) At the time of writing, Selena has 65 million Twitter followers.

(772) Selena is a fan of the Chai Latte from Starbucks.

Chai Latte is a spiced tea drink made with black tea, spices like cinnamon and clove, and milk.

(773) Selena is a fan of surfing.

(774) Selena says she is looking forward to turning thirty and says that getting older and growing-up has been much nicer than she expected. Selena says that one of the good things about getting older is that you become less sensitive to criticism and what people say about you.

(775) Selena is a fan of Smores. A smore is a famous treat consisting of one or more toasted marshmallows and a layer of chocolate sandwiched between two pieces of graham cracker.

(776) Only Murders in the Building earned four Critic's Choice Award nominations.

(777) Selena is set to produce a true crime docuseries titled Mi Vecino, El Cartel (The Cartel Among Us) for Univision's forthcoming subscription streaming service.

(778) Selena said she is impressed with the way Taylor Swift has stayed humble and down to earth despite her success.

(779) Selena says her family were so poor growing-up that they struggled to put gas in the car.

(780) Selena left Barney & Friends because she was too old for the show in the end. Child actors can obviously age out of parts pretty quick. They are changing all the time.

(781) Selena formed her own production company in 2008. She called it July Moon Productions.

(782) Selena played her Wizards character Alex Russo in a crossover episode of the Disney series The Suite Life on Deck.

(783) Selena worked with designers Tony Melillo and Sandra Campos on her fashion line Dream Out Loud.

(784) Selena said that one of her music and dance inspirations is Janet Jackson.

(785) The treatment center Selena went to was Dawn at The Meadows in Wickenburg, Arizona. Celebrities like Tiger Woods and Kate Moss have been treated there.

(786) Selena reprised the role of Mavis in Hotel Transylvania 2.

(787) Selena said that she wasn't really anything like her character Alex in Wizards of Waverley Place in real life. Selena said that Alex is a bit lazy and always getting into trouble but these are not qualities you could ascribe to her. Selena said the biggest similarity between her and Alex is that both are very outgoing.

(788) Taylor Swift and the actor Tom Hiddleston were seen together at a Selena concert in Nashville in 2016. At the time the pair were dating - although rumours persisted that their relationship was merely a fiendish marketing stunt cooked up by their publicists!

(789) In 2008, Selena was involved in St. Jude's Children's Hospital's "Runway For Life" benefit.

(790) In 2008, Selena was named UNICEF's spokesperson for the Trick-or-Treat for UNICEF campaign. This is a campaign that encourages children to

raise money for charity at Halloween. She took up this role again in 2009.

(791) Selena and Justin Bieber recorded an unreleased duet titled Can't Steal Our Love.

(792) In 2010, Selena featured as one of the two female leads in Ramona and Beezus, a film adaption of the children's novel series by Beverly Cleary.

(793) There have been sporadic rumours that Selena is in a relationship with Niall Horan but both have denied this. Selena says he is just a good friend.

(794) In 2020, Selena said it was quite scary releasing her first new music for two years because she was worried that people might have forgotten about her or that the album might flop. Selena said that anxieties like this are pretty common when you release something new. Fortunately, none of her music has flopped or forced her to question whether to continue with her music career.

(795) Selena is a fan of crop tops. She says she likes showing her shoulders off.

(796) When it comes to cars, Selena has owned a Porsche, BMW, and Ford Escape.

(797) Selena is a big fan of the sitcom Friends and has watched all the episodes more than once.

(798) Selena is a fan of the dark anthology show Black Mirror.

(799) Selena says that one of her biggest fashion icons is Natalie Portman.

(800) Selena said she doesn't post on her social media accounts herself though she oversees her content on these platforms. Selena prefers to have what you might describe as an arm's length relationship with social media. It is important for her charity work and career but on a personal level she can happily live without it.

(801) Selena is a fan of Christina Aguilera.

(802) Selena is a big fan of Billie Eilish.

(803) Selena said the fictional place she would most like to live is Wonderland from Alice's Adventures in Wonderland. She said that the Mad Hatter from this book is also the fictional character she would most like to spend a day with.

Alice's Adventures in Wonderland was published in 1865 and written by Lewis Carroll. Lewis Carroll was the pseudonym of Charles Dodgson. Dodgson was also a scholar, poet, and mathematician. He conjured up the adventures of Alice as a means to entertain the children of some friends during lazy summer days by the river. Once his fantastical tales were put into book form, Alice's Adventures in Wonderland eventually became of the most famous and enduring works of fiction ever published.

The book concerns a young girl named Alice who is dreamily sitting by a riverbank when she notices a white rabbit race past. Nothing strange about that you might think. However, this rabbit is wearing clothes and seems to keep checking a stopwatch as if time is of exceptional importance at this precise moment. Alice, naturally curious about this remarkable sight, explores but falls a down a rabbit hole into a strange world full of remarkable creatures who seem somewhat like the animals and insects of our world - only they can talk. It quickly transpires that logic plays little part in this topsy turvy and endlessly eccentric and strange world. But is it all a dream or is Alice really here?

Curiously, Alice's Adventures in Wonderland was not very well received when it first appeared and it was only after the publication of the sequel (Through the Looking Glass) that it got some traction and become much more loved and widely read. It's hard really to think of many more influential books than Alice's Adventures in Wonderland. It has inspired dozens of film and television adaptations and the image of little Alice in her blue dress is as identifiable as any character in fiction.

Alice's Adventures in Wonderland is a delight on every page and fantastically weird and offbeat. The book is a wonderful celebration of nonsense and whimsy and full of preposterous conversations, memorable characters, puzzles, poems, and enjoyable absurdity.

(804) Selena's early music career definitely got a big boost from her Disney background because Disney promoted her songs. In mitigation though Selena did secure work in the entertainment industry before she signed a Disney contract. It's not as if she has only ever worked for Disney.

(805) Selena received the American Latino Media Arts Award in 2009 for Wizards of Waverly Place.

(806) Selena has described herself as a bit of a couch potato.

(807) Selena said the worst part of doing a big concert is the waiting around before you go on stage because her

stomach is always full of butterflies and there are plenty
of nerves. She says that you just want to get on the stage
and start the show as soon as possible and once you do
this the nerves dissipate and you are fine.

(808) Selena said she would be happy to live in New York
one day.

(809) Selena is a fan of sparkling grapefruit water.

(810) Selena has shown support for the LGBT
community.

(811) Selena took part in Disney commercials to promote
safe driving.

(812) Selena said she was 'fat-shamed' by sad trolls when
her weight fluctuated during to Lupus.

(813) After her kidney transplant, Selena made a joke
online about drinking too much alcohol lately. A few
idiots naturally missed the joke and took her literally.

(814) Selena said that if you want a dog you should adopt
a shelter dog and give it a nice home.

(815) Selena's kidney transplant was very serious at one
point. She could actually have died.

(816) We Don't Talk Anymore (featuring Charlie Puth)
spent 21 weeks on the Billboard chart.

(817) Selena is a fan of the band 5th Harmony.

(818) Waverly Place is actually a real place in New York.
Selena said she had lunch there once.

(819) Visitors to Selena's Los Angeles home have said that it looks a bit like a ski lodge!

(820) Selena is a fan of jam and preserves.

(821) Selena has had nineteen top 40 hits in the United Kingdom.

(822) Rare peaked at number ten on Spotify Global.

(823) A Billboard poll had Lose You to Love Me as Selena's best song. It won just over 40% of the vote.

(824) Selena voiced Betsy, a friendly Maasai giraffe, in the 2020 Robert Downey Jr. fantasy film Dolittle. This film got terrible reviews.

(825) Selena has worn clothes designed by Alex Chung.

(826) Selena says she is proud of her last name and likes to think that she is a good role model for Latins.

(827) Selena said she was scared of thunderstorms when she was a kid. She said that reading up about thunderstorms made her less scared.

(828) Selena said in 2020 that she would no longer make 'sexy' or suggestive music videos because her six year-old half-sister Gracie didn't like them.

(829) Selena has suggested that she would like to have a romantic relationship that takes place completely out of the public eye. No prizes for guessing who this might be a reference to.

(830) Selena's kidney transplant operation took six hours.

(831) Selena said she never sets herself goals because
she'd only be disappointed if she didn't reach them.

(832) Selena has never been associated with a crazy party
lifestyle like some other celebrities we could mention.
She's been very well behaved as far as celebrities go.

(833) Selena had a pinball machine in one of her old
homes.

(834) Selena said she enjoys voicing Mavis Dracula and
would be happy to carry on doing the character.

(835) Selena said she would like to make more Spanish
language albums in the future.

(836) Selena has been a spokesperson for State Farm
Insurance.

(837) Selena teamed up with her mother Mandy Teefey
and Daniella Pierson to launch a new mental health
platform called Wondermind.

(838) Selena says she finds it easier to sing in Spanish
than to speak it. For her Spanish language album she had
lessons with a Spanish coach.

(839) Selena's clothes range includes jewelry.

(840) Taylor Swift is one of Selena's best friends. They
have performed together. Selena says that Taylor has
given her plenty of good advice about coping with fame
and celebrity - not to mention the music industry.

(841) Selena was up for a lead role in the 2011 film Snow
White and the Huntsman but lost out in the end to

Kristen Stewart.

(842) Selena said she would love to have done a duet with Elvis Presley.

(843) Selena likes to do yoga.

(844) Despite being a Friends superfan, Selena only got 11 out of 29 questions right when she took a Friends quiz.

(845) Selena enjoys skateboarding.

(846) Selena's favourite subject at school was science.

(847) Selena voiced Princess Selenia in the 2009 film Arthur and the Revenge of Maltazard.

(848) Selena is a fan of Dubai as a holiday destination.

(849) Selena has attended a CrimeCon convention. This is a place where true crime buffs can get together and investigate unsolved crimes.

(850) Selena says that when she wants to relax she takes a bath with Epsom salt. Epsom salt is said to have positive health benefits because it contains magnesium.

(851) As you might expect of someone who loves horror movies, Selena is a big fan of Halloween.

(852) Selena is a fan of Chipotle Mexican Grill. Chipotle Mexican Grill, Inc is an American chain of fast casual restaurants best known for tacos and Mission burritos that are made to order in front of the customer. The name derives from chipotle, the Nahuatl name for a smoked and dried jalapeño chili pepper.

(853) Selena is a fan of blackberries.

(854) Selena has had seven albums inside the top forty charts in the United Kingdom.

(855) Selena's song De Una Vez debuted with over 3 million streams on Spotify.

(856) When Selena visited London in 2019, she wore four different outfits in a single day!

(857) Selena had 2.6 billion streams on Spotify in 2021.

(858) Selena seems to be quite fond of gold trousers.

(859) Selena has over nineteen billion views on YouTube.

(860) Selena is a fan of California Tortilla. California Tortilla, also known as Cal Tort, is an American chain of franchised fast casual Mexican-style restaurants.

(861) Selena has served as a spokesperson for Louis Vuitton.

(862) Selena's favourite horror movies include Child's Play, Psycho, Haunt, Orphan, and Insidious.

(863) Selena was friends with the Glee star Corey Monteith. Sadly, Corey died in 2013 at the age of 31. They acted together in the film Monte Carlo.

(864) Selena apparently doesn't believe in diets and weighing yourself. She just thinks you have to stay active and try to eat healthy food.

(865) Selena says she would describe herself as a

perfectionist.

(866) Selena is a fan of McDonald's. Her staple order is a Ranch BLT with either grilled or crispy chicken and fries.

(867) Luxury accessories and handbag brand Coach paid Selena $10 million to promote their products in 2016.

(868) Selena thinks that the crust is the best part of a pizza. You might describe this as rather eccentric.

(869) Selena is a fan of teriyaki sauce. The primary ingredients of this sauce include soy sauce, brown sugar, garlic, ginger, honey and mirin.

(870) Selena says she cringes a bit sometimes when she looks back at her very early music and fashion.

(871) Lose You To Love Me spent 27 weeks on the Billboard chart.

(872) Revelación ranked fifth on Itunes in 2021 when it came to female projects.

(873) Only Murders in the Building has a perfect 100% score on Rotten Tomatoes.

(874) Selena and DJ Snake's Selfish Love was certified gold in France for the amount of units sold.

(875) Voters on FanPop voted Kiss & Tell as the best song on Naturally.

(876) Selena owns some Sergio Rossi sandals.

(877) Selena has a beige Manning Cartell coat.

(878) Selena has been seen wearing denim quite a lot.

(879) Selena was seen in New York wearing an Alexandre Vautheir asymmetrical dress in 2017.

(880) Selena was seen sporting a pink Miu Miu top and pants in 2017.

(881) Selena likes Christopher Kane dresses.

(882) Selena likes Isabel Marant dresses.

(883) Selena likes pink vanilla ice cream.

(884) You could probably describe Selena as quite a private person although you certainly wouldn't say she was enigmatic or reclusive.

(885) Selena said if she had to something other than an actor and singer she would like to be a chef.

(886) Selena has an endorsement deal with Louis Vuitton.

(887) Selena is a fan of blueberries.

(888) Selena is generally regarded to be a dance-pop artist when it comes to music.

(889) Selena is a fan of Oreo cookies.

(890) Selena made an appearance in the 2016 comedy sequel Neighbors 2: Sorority Rising. This film got quite good reviews.

(891) Selena's Serendipity 3 sundae for charity was a spin

on cookies and cream.

(892) Selena thinks she can make a mean omelet.

(893) Selena is a fan of Popeyes. Popeyes Louisiana Kitchen, Inc., also known as Popeyes and formerly named Popeyes Chicken & Biscuits and Popeyes Famous Fried Chicken & Biscuits, is an American multinational chain of fried chicken fast food restaurants that was founded in 1972 in New Orleans, Louisiana and headquartered in Miami, Florida.

(894) Selena was quite overwhelmed when she actually met Shia Lebouf for the first time.

(896) Selena has performed on The Ellen DeGeneres Show.

(897) An article on Mashable said that in a poll 85% of people who watched Selena's cooking show said she couldn't cook. This poll seemed rather pointless because the whole point of the show is that Selena is learning how to cook!

(898) Selena is a fan of romantic candlelit dinners.

(899) Selena has suggested that her relationship with Justin Bieber was emotionally abusive at times.

(900) Selena said she is not bothered by the perception of her through the rarefied prism of social media and celebrity culture because this is a false image.

(901) When Selena was making Only Murders in the building she rented an apartment in New York.

(902) Justin Bieber's song Ghost (which is about a lost love) is alleged to be about Selena.

(903) Selena is a big fan of cherries.

(904) Selena's first duties for UNICEF involved a trip to Ghana.

(905) Selena said that Crazy, Stupid, Love is one of her favourite movies.

(906) The sunglasses Selena had on in her Hit the Lights music video were the same glasses that she wore in Wizards of Waverly Place: The Movie.

(907) Selena has done a duet with Coldplay.

(908) It is sometimes said that, despite famously playing a wizard herself, Selena doesn't like Harry Potter. This doesn't ring true though because she was once seen enjoying herself at the Wizarding World of Harry Potter theme park.

(909) Selena was the voice of Steve Carrell's daughter in Horton Hears a Who but she never actually met him recording her lines for the film. She only met him months later.

(910) Selena performed for the BBC's charity event Children in Need in 2015.

(911) Although it probably isn't very good for her, Selena says she drinks coffee nearly every day.

(912) Selena said that she finds social media weird because the Selena Gomez image projected on places like

Instagram isn't really the real her. It's all an image and facade.

(913) Selena is a big fan of pretzels.

(914) Selena is a fan of Cheryl Cole. Cheryl Cole is an English singer who used to be in Girls Aloud.

(915) In 2018, Selena's Instagram posted a picture of her holding a red cocktail while relaxing in a low cut black dress. The photo became her most liked ever picture on Instagram and got ten million likes. However, she then deleted it. Why did she delete it? No one knows but in a cryptic response Selena said she doesn't actually post and delete on Instagram herself. She has others do this.

(916) Selena likes spicy food and always has peppers in her kitchen.

(917) Selena is a fan of Moe's. Moe's is an American fast casual restaurant franchise chain that was founded in Atlanta, Georgia. Moe's offers burritos, tacos, quesadillas, nachos, salads, stacks, burrito bowls, and house-made seasonal salsas.

(918) In 2018, Selena said she had no apps on her phone apart from a little puzzle game.

(919) Selena has worked with stylist Basha Richard since she was a teenager.

(920) According to SocialBlade.Com, Selena's YouTube channel is the 37th most viewed YouTube channel in the United States.

(921) Selena is a fan of Thai food.

(922) Selena has around 40 million followers on TikTok.

(923) Selena starred in a 2014 comedy called film called Behaving Badly. The film ended up going to straight to video on demand and got poor reviews.

(924) There was press speculation a few years go that Justin Bieber had tried to reach out to Selena and regretted the way their relationship ended.

(925) Selena said she would like to have the magic power to make food appear on her table whenever she is hungry!

(926) Selena's song Come & Get It won an MTV Music Video award.

(927) Selena says she has always been a bit scared of the ocean.

(928) Selena is a fan of deep dish pizzas.

(929) An old poll on PopCrush ranked The Heart Wants What It Wants as Selena's best song. It took 16% of the vote.

(930) Selena says she dislikes Sauerkraut. Sauerkraut is a fermented cabbage dish that comes from Germany.

(931) Selena tried some Vegemite on her cooking show and found it revolting. Vegemite is an Australian yeast spread. The British yeast spread Marmite is more or less the same thing. In fact, 'Marmite' is a popular expression in Britain to describe something you'll either love or hate. It seems that Selena was firmly in the hate category when it comes to yeast spreads!

(932) The second official Selena Gomez fragrance was Vivamore Selena Gomez for women. This fragrance has top notes of melon and white tea.

(933) Selena is a fan of Skrillex.

(934) It is said that, as a romantic gesture in 2011, Justin Bieber booked the entire Staples Center in Los Angeles so that he and Selena could watch the film Titanic together!

(935) Selena supports the charity Raise Hope for Congo. This is a charity that seeks to help woman who have been subjected to violence.

(936) Selena owns some Stuart Weitzman sandals.

(937) Selena describes her own fashion style as bohemian.

(938) Thetoptens.com ranked Selena as the greatest ever Disney Channel star. Zendaya was ranked second.

(939) A 2022 article on Collider ranked Wizards of Waverly Place as the ninth greatest ever Disney Channel show. The top spot went to K.C. Undercover.

(940) Selena and Justin Bieber wore coordinated outfits when they made their first public appearance together as a couple. You could say that a lot of thought went into that appearance!
(941) At the 2017 British Fashion Awards, Selena wore a white lace dress by Coach.

(942) Selena says she was shy as a kid but she certainly seemed super confident in her Disney audition.

(943) Selena was seen in a black Proenza Schouler dress in 2017.

(944) One of Selena's nicknames is Sel.

(945) Selena seems to be a fan of platform boots.

(946) Wizards of Waverly Place has a rating of 6.9/10 on IMDB.

(947) Selena says that doing accents is much harder than learning lines. This is doubtless a reference to her role in Monte Carlo.

(948) Selena often matches a dress with white sneakers.

(949) Selena has a Gerard Darel wide-brim hat.

(950) Selena enjoys baking cupcakes.

(951) In 2015, Selena dated DJ and music producer Zedd.

(952) Selena has performed on Late Night with Jimmy Fallon.

(953) Selena likes Victor Glemaud dresses.

(954) In 2013, Selena visited Levine Children's Hospital in Charlotte, NC during the Stars Dance Tour.

(955) Selena seems quite fond of wearing white loafers.

(956) Selena is a fan of Tom Petty and the Heartbreakers.

(957) At the 2017 Lupus Research Alliance Gala in NYC, Selena wore a yellow Calvin Klein dress.

(958) Selena was seen rocking a velvet feather-trimmed coat covered in crystals by Miu Miu while in Paris in 2019.

(959) Selena has an AC/DC (a heavy metal band) t-shirt.

(960) Selena says she would probably describe herself as a shopoholic.

(961) Selena owns a blue Prius Prime car.

(962) Selena is a fan of watermelon - especially in the summer.

(963) Selena is a fan of the Bronco Burrito eating establishment.

(964) In 2021, voters on Ranker.Com voted Selena the 41st most beautiful woman in the world.

(965) The song Naturally gave Selena Gomez & the Scene their first top ten hit in the United Kingdom.

(966) Selena's English-speaking studio albums have sold over five million copies combined. Her biggest sales markets are the United States and Latin America. She has sold pretty well in Europe too - especially the United Kingdom.

(967) Ice Cream, Selena's song with Blackpink, sold around one and a half million downloads. Many of these came from the increasingly lucrative Chinese market.

(968) The singer Charlie Puth said that he dated Selena in 2016.

(969) Selena said she enjoyed Only Murders in the Building because it was a rare case of her playing a character her own age. For many roles in her career she has had to play someone younger.

(970) Selena said that when she was a child actor she was very good at learning lines. This was obviously something that helped a lot when it came to getting work.

(971) Selena's first fragrance came in a very distinct long narrow purple body with lips depicted above the lid.

(972) Selena's first fragrance has an average rating of 4.7 out of 5 on Amazon.

(973) Selena was judged the highest paid actress in 2014. One must remember though that her commercial deals and music contributed generously to her earnings. It wasn't as if she made $96 million from a couple of movies!

(974) Voters on Ranker.Com have Love You Like A Love Song as Selena's best music video. This song was of course from the Selena Gomez & the Scene days.

(975) Selena says she is a big fan of her grandmother's corn casserole.

(976) Selena was voted Favorite Pop/Rock Female Artist in 2016 by the AMA.

(977) Selena described her own personally designed fragrance as yummy.

(978) Selena was one of but many celebrities to express dismay for President Trump.

(979) Selena thinks her music became better and more meaningful after her friend Taylor Swift advised her to write about her own life and experiences in the lyrics.

(980) A number of former child Disney stars have had their careers (tragically in some cases) burn out early so one could say that Selena's stability and longevity is an impressive achievement.

(981) Selena thinks she can rap a bit - but only for fun. We shouldn't hold our breath waiting for a Selena Gomez rap album!

(982) Selena says that when it comes to her work and even business life that she will only commit to something that feels authentic and meaningful.

(983) A poll on FanPop rated Rare as Selena's best solo album.

(984) Selena said she was very reluctant to ask anyone to donate a kidney and never actually did this - not even family members. Thankfully though her friend Francia Raisa volunteered without being asked.

(985) Selena is a fan of Subway sandwiches.

(986) Selena is said to like eating flounder. This is a type of flat fish.

(987) The Selena Sundae at Serendipity 3 received some criticism for costing $30. That's a lot of money for an ice cream!

(988) Selena is a fan of the MAC eye shadow Naked Lunch.

(989) Selena wore a Christian Coda dress for the Kids Choice Awards in 2011.

(990) Selena is a fan of iced coffee.

(991) Selena has some Jennifer Fisher hoop earrings

(992) Selena seems to be fond of wearing suits. Among the designs she likes are pinstripe and blue satin.

(993) Selena says she has become more forthright and opinionated as she has become older.

(994) Selena said that she never looks at Instagram on her phone.

(995) Selena said she is eternally thankful that her grandparents made it across the border and paved the way for her to be born in the United States.

(996) Selena is a fan of the Clarisonic Sonic Radiance Skin Renewing Peel Wash.

(997) Selena's family remain very much a part of her team.

(998) In 2014, Selena said she wouldn't change being a former Disney kid for anything in the world.

(999) Selena said that the cast and crew on Wizards of Waverly Place were like a family to her.

(1000) Taylor Swift says that Selena is the most honest person she has ever met.

Discography

Studio albums

Stars Dance

July 19, 2013
Label: Hollywood
CD, LP, digital download, streaming

Revival

October 9, 2015
Label: Interscope
CD, LP, digital download, streaming

Rare

January 10, 2020
Label: Interscope
CD, LP, digital download, cassette, streaming

Compilation albums

For You

November 24, 2014
Label: Hollywood
CD, digital download, streaming

Love You Like a Love Song, Come & Get It, and More

August 20, 2021
Label: UMG Recordings
Streaming

Extended plays

Another Cinderella Story

June 16, 2009
Label: Razor & Tie
Digital download

For You

January 1, 2015
Label: Hollywood
Streaming

Selena × Votes

October 30, 2020
Label: Interscope
Digital download, streaming

Revelación

March 12, 2021
Label: Interscope

CD, LP, digital download, cassette, streaming

Singles

As lead artist

2008

Tell Me Something I Don't Know

2009

Magic

2013

Come & Get It

Slow Down

2014

The Heart Wants What It Wants

2015

Good for You

Same Old Love

2016

Hands to Myself

Kill Em with Kindness

It Ain't Me

Bad Liar

Fetish

Wolves

2019

I Can't Get Enough

Lose You to Love Me

Look at Her Now

2020

Rare

Boyfriend

Past Life (Remix)

Ice Cream

2021

De Una Vez

Baila Conmigo

Selfish Love

999

As featured artist

2009

**Whoa Oh! (Me vs. Everyone)(Remix)
(Forever the Sickest Kids featuring Selena
Gomez)**

2015

**I Want You to Know
(Zedd featuring Selena Gomez)**

2016

**We Don't Talk Anymore
(Charlie Puth featuring Selena Gomez)**

**Hands
(among various artists)**

**Trust Nobody
(Cashmere Cat featuring Selena Gomez and Tory
Lanez)**

2018

**Taki Taki
(DJ Snake featuring Selena Gomez, Ozuna and
Cardi B)**

2019

**Anxiety
(Julia Michaels featuring Selena Gomez)**

Promotional singles

2009

**Send It On
(with Miley Cyrus, Jonas Brothers and Demi
Lovato)**

2010

Shake It Up

2015

Me & the Rhythm
2020

Feel Me

Other charted songs

2009

**New Classic
(with Drew Seeley)**

**One and the Same
(with Demi Lovato)**

2012

**Bidi Bidi Bom Bom
(with Selena)**

2013

Birthday

Stars Dance

2015

Sober

Me & My Girls

2017

Only You

2020

Dance Again

Ring

Vulnerable

People You Know

Let Me Get Me

**Crowded Room
(featuring 6lack)**

Souvenir

2021

Buscando Amor

**Dámelo To
(featuring Myke Towers)**

**Vicio
Adios**

**Let Somebody Go
(with Coldplay)**

Filmography

2003

Spy Kids 3-D: Game Over Water Park Girl

2008

Another Cinderella Story Mary Santiago

Horton Hears a Who! Helga (voice)

2009

Arthur and the Revenge of Maltazard Princess Selenia (voice)

2010

Ramona and Beezus Beatrice "Beezus" Quimby

Arthur 3: The War of the Two Worlds Princess Selenia (voice)

2011

Monte Carlo Grace Ann Bennett / Cordelia Winthrop Scott

The Muppets Herself

2012

Fifty Shades of Blue Herself / Lauren (voice) Short film

Spring Breakers Faith

Hotel Transylvania Mavis Dracula (voice)

Aftershock   VIP Girl

2013

Getaway The Kid

Girl Rising Narrator (voice)

Searching Violet

2014

Rudderless   Kate Ann Lucas

Behaving Badly Nina Pennington

2015

Unity   **Narrator** (voice)

Hotel Transylvania 2 Mavis (voice)

The Big Short Herself

Taylor Swift: The 1989 World Tour Live

2016

The Fundamentals of Caring Dot

Neighbors 2: Sorority Rising Phi Lambda President
In Dubious Battle Lisa

2017

Puppy! Mavis (voice)

2018

A Love Story Girl

Hotel Transylvania 3: Summer Vacation Mavis
(voice)

2019

The Dead Don't Die Zoe

A Rainy Day in New York Chan Tyrell

2020

Dolittle Betsy (voice)

2022

Hotel Transylvania: Transformania Mavis (voice)

In the Shadow of the Mountain Silvia Vasquez-Lavado

Photo Credit

https://commons.wikimedia.org/wiki/File:Selena_Gome
z_-_Walmart_Soundcheck_Concert.jpg

22 July 2013

Author Lunchbox LP, Culver City, California